AF891394

CIMA®

## How to access your online resources

Kaplan Financial students will have a MyKaplan account and these extra resources will be available to you online. You do not need to register again, as this process was completed when you enrolled. If you are having problems accessing online materials, please ask your course administrator.

If you are not studying with Kaplan and did not purchase your book via a Kaplan website, to unlock your extra online resources please go to **www.mykaplan.co.uk/add-online-resources** (even if you have set up an account and registered books previously). You will then need to enter the ISBN number (on the title page and back cover) and the unique pass key number contained in the scratch panel below to gain access.

You will also be required to enter additional information during this process to set up or confirm your account details.

If you purchased through the Kaplan Publishing website you will automatically receive an e-mail invitation to register your details and gain access to your content. If you do not receive the e-mail or book content, please contact Kaplan Publishing.

This code can only be used once for the registration of this book online. This registration and your online content will expire when the examinations covered by this book have taken place. Please allow one hour from the time you submit your book details for us to process your request.

**Please scratch the film to access your unique code.**

Please be aware that this code is case-sensitive and you will need to include the dashes within the passcode, but not when entering the ISBN.

KAPLAN PUBLISHING

CIMA's CGMA® 2019 Professional Examinations

# CIMA'S CGMA Management Level

## Subject E2

---

## Managing Performance

---

## EXAM PRACTICE KIT

CIMA™

KAPLAN PUBLISHING

Published by: Kaplan Publishing UK

Unit 2 The Business Centre, Molly Millars Lane, Wokingham, Berkshire RG41 2QZ



## Acknowledgements

We are grateful to the CIMA for permission to reproduce past examination questions. The answers to CIMA Exams have been prepared by Kaplan Publishing, except in the case of the CIMA November 2010 and subsequent CIMA Exam answers where the official CIMA answers have been reproduced. Questions from past live assessments have been included by kind permission of CIMA.

## Notice

The text in this material and any others made available by any Kaplan Group company does not amount to advice on a particular matter and should not be taken as such. No reliance should be placed on the content as the basis for any investment or other decision or in connection with any advice given to third parties. Please consult your appropriate professional adviser as necessary.

Kaplan Publishing Limited and all other Kaplan group companies expressly disclaim all liability to any person in respect of any losses or other claims, whether direct, indirect, incidental, consequential or otherwise arising in relation to the use of such materials.

Kaplan is not responsible for the content of external websites. The inclusion of a link to a third party website in this text should not be taken as an endorsement.

Kaplan Publishing's learning materials are designed to help students succeed in their examinations. In certain circumstances, CIMA can make post-exam adjustment to a student's mark or grade to reflect adverse circumstances which may have disadvantaged a student's ability to take an exam or demonstrate their normal level of attainment (see CIMA's Special Consideration policy). However, it should be noted that students will not be eligible for special consideration by CIMA if preparation for or performance in a CIMA exam is affected by any failure by their tuition provider to prepare them properly for the exam for any reason including, but not limited to, staff shortages, building work or a lack of facilities etc.

Similarly, CIMA will not accept applications for special consideration on any of the following grounds:

- failure by a tuition provider to cover the whole syllabus
- failure by the student to cover the whole syllabus, for instance as a result of joining a course part way through
- failure by the student to prepare adequately for the exam, or to use the correct pre-seen material
- errors in the Kaplan Official Study Text, including sample (practice) questions or any other Kaplan content or
- errors in any other study materials (from any other tuition provider or publisher).

## British Library Cataloguing in Publication Data

A catalogue record for this book is available from the British Library.

ISBN: 978-1-83735-104-6

Printed and bound in Great Britain

# CONTENTS



Quality and accuracy are of the utmost importance to us so if you spot an error in any of our products, please send an email to mykaplanreporting@kaplan.com with full details.

Our Quality Co-ordinator will work with our technical team to verify the error and take action to ensure it is corrected in future editions.

# INDEX TO QUESTIONS AND ANSWERS

## OBJECTIVE TEST QUESTIONS

# EXAM TECHNIQUES

## COMPUTER-BASED ASSESSMENT

### Golden rules

1 Make sure you have completed the compulsory 15-minute tutorial before you start the test. This tutorial is available through the AICPA & CIMA website and focusses on the functionality of the exam. You cannot speak to the invigilator once you have started.

2 These exam practice kits give you plenty of exam style questions to practise so make sure you use them to fully prepare.

3 Attempt all questions, there is no negative marking.

4 Double check your answer before you put in the final answer although you can change your response as many times as you like.

5 Not all questions will be multiple choice questions (MCQs) – you may have to fill in missing words or figures.

6 Identify the easy questions first and get some points on the board to build up your confidence.

7 Attempt 'wordy' questions first as these may be quicker than the computation style questions. This will relieve some of the time pressure you will be under during the exam.

8 If you don't know the answer, flag the question and attempt it later. In your final review before the end of the exam try a process of elimination.

9 Work out your answer on the whiteboard provided first if it is easier for you. There is also an onscreen 'scratch pad' on which you can make notes. You are not allowed to take pens, pencils, rulers, pencil cases, phones, paper or notes into the testing room.

# SYLLABUS GUIDANCE, LEARNING OBJECTIVES AND VERBS

## A CIMA's CGMA® 2019 PROFESSIONAL QUALIFICATION

Details regarding the content of the CIMA's CGMA 2019 professional qualification can be located within the CGMA 2019 professional qualification syllabus document.

You can use the following diagram showing the whole structure of your qualification to help you keep track of your progress. Make sure you seek appropriate advice if you are unsure about your progression through the qualification.

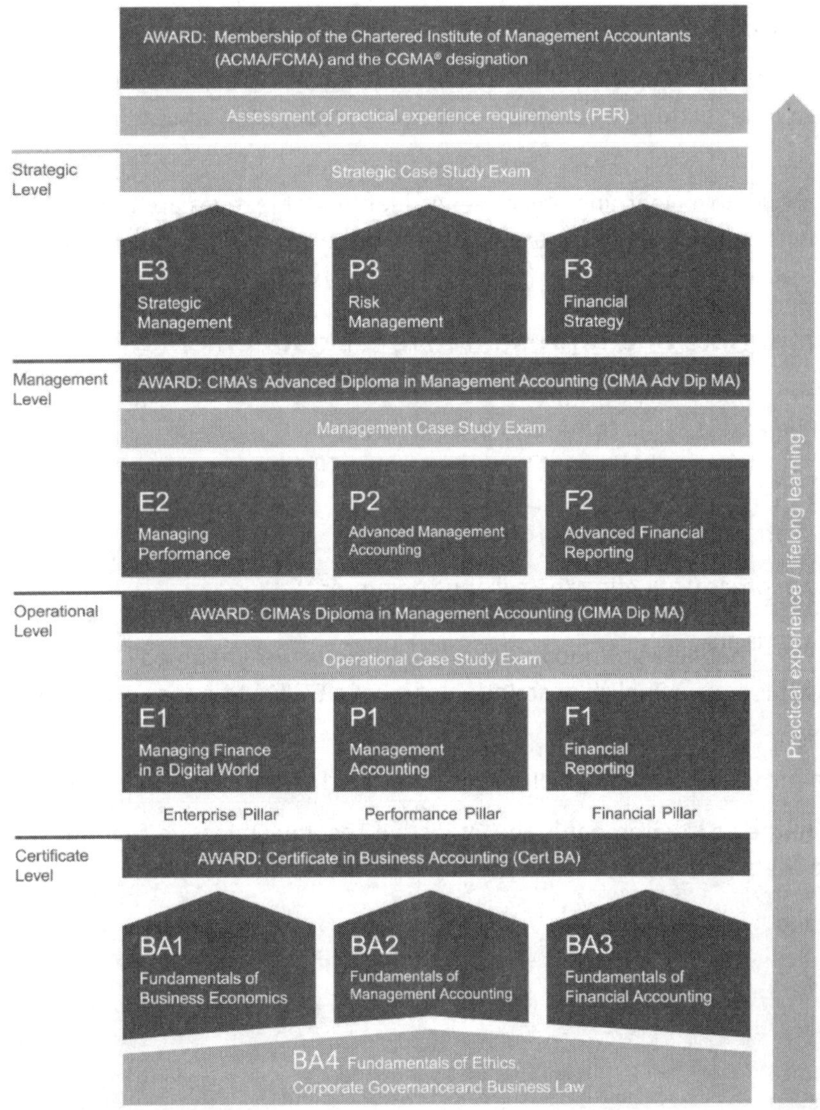


Reproduced with CIMA's permission

# B STUDY WEIGHTINGS

A percentage weighting is shown against each exam content area in CIMA's CGMA® Exam Blueprints. This is intended as a guide to the proportion of study time each topic requires.

All component learning outcomes will be tested.

The weightings do not specify the number of marks that will be allocated to topics in the examination.

# C LEARNING OUTCOMES

Each subject within the qualification is divided into a number of broad syllabus topics. The topics contain one or more lead learning outcomes, related component learning outcomes and indicative knowledge content.

A learning outcome has two main purposes:

1 to define the skill or ability that a well-prepared candidate should be able to exhibit in the examination

2 to demonstrate the approach likely to be taken by examiners in examination questions.

The learning outcomes are part of a hierarchy of learning objectives. The verbs used at the beginning of each learning outcome relate to a specific learning objective, e.g. Evaluate alternative approaches to budgeting.

The verb 'evaluate' indicates a high-level learning objective. As learning objectives are hierarchical, it is expected that at this level students will have knowledge of different budgeting systems and methodologies and be able to apply them.

## CIMA's CGMA Exam Blueprints and representative task statements

CIMA have also published examination blueprints giving learners clear expectations regarding what is expected of them. This can be accessed via the AICPA & CIMA website.

The blueprint is structured as follows:

- Exam content sections (reflecting the syllabus document)
- Lead and component outcomes (reflecting the syllabus document)
- Representative task statements.

A representative task statement is a plain English description of what a CGMA® finance professional should know and be able to do.

The content and skill level determine the language and verbs used in the representative task.

CIMA will test up to the level of the task statement in the Objective Test (an Objective Test question on a particular topic could be set at a lower level than the task statement in the blueprint).

The task statements in the blueprint are representative and are not intended to be (nor should they be viewed as) an all-inclusive list of tasks that may be tested on the Examination. It also should be noted that the number of tasks associated with a particular content group or topic is not indicative of the extent such content group, topic or related skill level will be assessed on the test.

The format of the Objective Test blueprints follows that of the published syllabus for the 2019 CIMA Professional Qualification.

Weightings for content sections are also included in the individual subject blueprints.

A list of the learning objectives and the verbs that appear in the syllabus learning outcomes and examinations follows and these will help you to understand the depth and breadth required for a topic and the skill level the topic relates to.

## CIMA's verb hierarchy

| Skill level | Verbs used | Definition |
|---|---|---|
| **Level 5**<br>**Evaluation**<br>How you are expected to use your learning to evaluate, make decisions or recommendations | Advise | Counsel, inform or notify |
| | Assess | Evaluate or estimate the nature, ability or quality of |
| | Evaluate | Appraise or assess the value of |
| | Recommend | Propose a course of action |
| | Review | Assess and evaluate in order, to change if necessary |
| **Level 4**<br>**Analysis**<br>How you are expected to analyse the detail of what you have learned | Align | Arrange in an orderly way |
| | Analyse | Examine in detail the structure of |
| | Communicate | Share or exchange information |
| | Compare and contrast | Show the similarities and/or differences between |
| | Develop | Grow and expand a concept |
| | Discuss | Examine in detail by argument |
| | Examine | Inspect thoroughly |
| | Interpret | Translate into intelligible or familiar terms |
| | Monitor | Observe and check the progress of |
| | Prioritise | Place in order of priority or sequence for action |
| | Produce | Create or bring into existence |
| **Level 3**<br>**Application**<br>How you are expected to apply your knowledge | Apply | Put to practical use |
| | Calculate | Ascertain or reckon mathematically |
| | Conduct | Organise and carry out |
| | Demonstrate | Prove with certainty or exhibit by practical means |
| | Prepare | Make or get ready for use |
| | Reconcile | Make or prove consistent/compatible |
| **Level 2**<br>**Comprehension**<br>What you are expected to understand | Describe | Communicate the key features of |
| | Distinguish | Highlight the differences between |
| | Explain | Make clear or intelligible/state the meaning or purpose of |
| | Identify | Recognise, establish or select after consideration |
| | Illustrate | Use an example to describe or explain something |
| **Level 1**<br>**Knowledge**<br>What you are expected to know | List | Make a list of |
| | State | Express, fully or clearly, the details/facts of |
| | Define | Give the exact meaning of |
| | Outline | Give a summary of |

# D OBJECTIVE TEST

## Objective Test

Objective Test questions require you to choose or provide a response to a question whose correct answer is predetermined.

The most common types of Objective Test question you will see are:

- Multiple choice, where you have to choose the correct answer(s) from a list of possible answers. This could either be numbers or text.
- Multiple response, for example, choosing two correct answers from a list of eight possible answers. This could either be numbers or text.
- Fill in the blank, where you fill in your answer within the provided space.
- Drag and drop, for example, matching a technical term with the correct definition.
- Hot spots, where you select an answer by clicking on graphs/diagrams.

## Guidance re CIMA's on-screen calculator

As part of the CGMA objective test software, candidates are now provided with a calculator. This calculator is on-screen and is available for the duration of the assessment. The calculator is available in each of the Objective Tests and is accessed by clicking the calculator button in the top left hand corner of the screen at any time during the assessment. Candidates are permitted to utilise personal calculators as long as they are an approved CIMA model. CIMA approved model list can be found on the AICPA & CIMA website.

All candidates must complete a 15-minute exam tutorial before the assessment begins and will have the opportunity to familiarise themselves with the calculator and practise using it. The exam tutorial is also available online via the AICPA & CIMA website. Candidates can use their own calculators providing it is included in CIMA's authorised calculator listing.

## Fundamentals of Objective Tests

The Objective Tests are 90-minute assessments comprising 60 compulsory questions, with one or more parts. There will be no choice and all questions should be attempted. All elements of a question must be answered correctly for the question to be marked correctly. All questions are equally weighted.

# APPROACH TO REVISION

## Stage 1: Assess areas of strengths and weaknesses

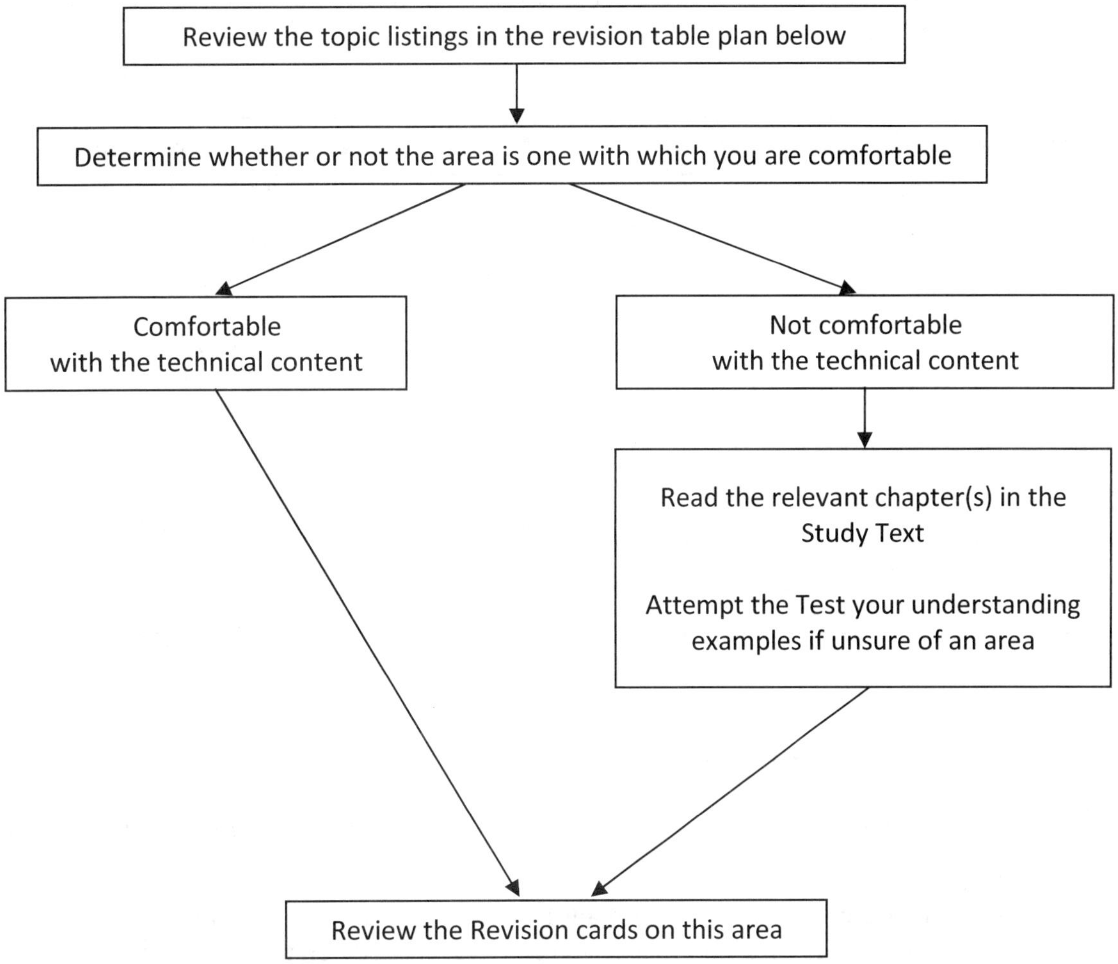

## Stage 2: Question practice

Follow the order of revision of topics as recommended in the revision table plan below and attempt the questions in the order suggested.

Try to avoid referring to text books and notes and the model answer until you have completed your attempt.

Try to answer the question in the allotted time.

Review your attempt with the model answer and assess how much of the answer you achieved in the allocated exam time.

Comfortable with question attempt

→ Only revisit when comfortable with questions on all topic areas

Not comfortable with question attempts

→ Focus on these areas by:

- Reworking Test your understanding examples in the Study Text
- Revisiting the technical content from the Revision cards
- Working any remaining questions on that area in the Exam Practice Kit
- Reattempting an exam standard question in that area, on a timed, closed book basis

## Stage 3: Final pre-exam revision

We recommend that you **attempt at least one ninety minute mock examination** containing a set of previously unseen exam standard questions.

It is important that you get a feel for the breadth of coverage of a real exam without advanced knowledge of the topic areas covered – just as you will expect to see on the real exam day.

Ideally a mock examination offered by your tuition provider should be sat in timed, closed book, real exam conditions.

# CGMA SYLLABUS GRIDS

## E2: Managing Performance

### Mechanisms to implement decisions and manage people performance

**Content weighting**

| | Content area | Weighting |
|---|---|---|
| A | Business models and value creation | 30% |
| B | Managing people performance | 40% |
| C | Managing projects | 30% |
| | | **100%** |

# E2A: Business models and value creation

The digital world is characterised by disruptions to business models by new entrants and incumbents who seek superior performance and competitive advantage. This section covers the fundamentals of business models and how new business and operating models can be developed to improve the performance of organisations.

| Lead outcome | Component outcome | Topics to be covered | Explanatory notes |
|---|---|---|---|
| 1. Explain the ecosystems of organisations.. | Explain:<br>a. Markets and competition<br>b. Society and regulation | • Definition of ecosystems<br>• Participants and roles<br>• Interactions and dynamics<br>• Rules and governance<br>• Technology<br>• Risks and opportunities | What is the nature of the ecosystem? What are its critical elements and how do they interact with each other? How do they impact the organisation? |
| 2. Explain the elements of business models. | Explain the following<br>a. Concept of value and the business model<br>b. Defining value<br>c. Creating value<br>d. Delivering value<br>e. Capturing and sharing value | • Stakeholders and relevant value<br>• Stakeholder analysis<br>• Resources, process, activities and people in creating value<br>• Products, services, customer segments, channels and platforms to deliver value<br>• Distribution of value to key stakeholders | This section covers the concept of value from different stakeholder perspectives. It examines the various elements of the business model, their interaction<br>with each other and their implication for costs and revenue. The section also covers the connectivity and alignment between the ecosystem and the elements of the business model. |
| 3. Analyse new business models in digital ecosystems. | a. Analyse digital business models and their related operating models | • Disruption<br>• Ways to build disruptive and resilient business models<br>• Creating digital operating models<br>• Types of digital operating models | New business models have evolved to disrupt industries and their ecosystems. What are they? How have they redefined their industries? |

## E2B: Managing people performance

Human capital is one of the key intangible assets of organisations in an age where intangible assets are the dominant means by which organisations create and preserve value. Leadership is a crucial means for managing individual performance and the relationships between people. This section examines how different styles of leadership can be used to improve the performance of individuals so they can achieve organisational goals.

| Lead outcome | Component outcome | Topics to be covered | Explanatory notes |
|---|---|---|---|
| 1. Compare and contrast different types of leadership and management styles. | Compare and contrast:<br>a. Different leadership concepts<br>b. Types of leadership<br>c. Leadership in different contexts | • Power, authority, delegation and empowerment<br>• Contingent and situational leadership<br>• Transactional and transformational leadership<br>• Leadership of virtual teams<br>• Leadership and ethics | Leadership is key to performance management. In a digital world it is an area that is least susceptible to automation. What constitutes leadership? What are the different types of leadership? How does one choose a style of leadership that is appropriate for the particular context? |
| 2. Analyse individual and team performance. | Analyse the following:<br>a. Employee performance objective setting<br>b. Employee appraisals<br>c. Coaching and mentoring<br>d. Managing workplace environment | • Target setting and employee alignment<br>• Employee empowerment and engagement<br>• Performance reporting and review<br>• Rewards and sanctions in managing performance<br>• Different approaches to coaching and mentoring to improve performance<br>• Diversity and equity practices<br>• Health and safety<br>• Organisational culture | Individual performance is achieved through structured processes and approaches. These include objective setting and regular review of performance against objectives. How should these processes be developed to ensure employee engagement, empowerment and alignment? How should the work environment be configured to enhance performance? What is the role of the leader in coaching and mentoring for high performance? |
| 3. Explain how to manage relationships. | Explain the following in the context of managing relationships:<br>a. Building and leading teams<br>b. Communications<br>c. Negotiations<br>d. Managing conflicts | • Characteristics of high-performing teams<br>• Motivating team members<br>• Communication process<br>• Digital tools for communication<br>• Negotiation process<br>• Strategies for negotiation<br>• Sources and types of conflicts<br>• Strategies for managing conflicts<br>• Leadership and ethics | Individuals work in teams and their performance contributes to the team performance. How should teams be built and led to improve performance? How is collaboration enhanced using technology? How can conflicts be managed? |

# E2C: Managing projects

Projects have become pervasive means by which organisations execute their strategies. This section shows candidates how to use project management concepts and techniques to implement strategies effectively and efficiently. It is linked to capital investment decision-making that is covered in other areas of the Management Level.

| Lead outcome | Component outcome | Topics to be covered | Explanatory notes |
|---|---|---|---|
| 1. Describe the concepts and phases of projects. | Describe the following:<br>a. Project objectives<br>b. Key stages of the project life cycle<br>c. Project control | • Overall project objectives<br>• Objectives relating to time, cost and quality<br>• Purpose and activities associated with key stages of the project life cycle | Projects are the primary means by which many organisations implement strategic decisions. It is also how organisations ensure cross-functional collaboration. This section covers the key elements of project management. It seeks to provide both awareness and understanding of the project management process and the ability to apply tools and techniques to participate in projects and to identify, evaluate and manage project risks. The objective is not to train project managers but to equip finance people to work within projects and to lead some parts of projects. |
| 2. Apply tools and techniques to manage projects. | Apply the following to manage projects:<br>a. Project management tools and techniques<br>b. Project risk management tools | • Workstreams<br>• Work breakdown schedule, Gantt charts, network analysis<br>• PERT charts<br>• Sources and types of project risks<br>• Scenario planning<br>• Managing project risks<br>• Project management software | |
| 3. Explain the concepts of project leadership. | Explain<br>a. Project structure<br>b. Roles of key project personnel<br>c. How to manage project stakeholders | • Project structures and their impact on project performance<br>• Role of project manager<br>• Role of key members of project team<br>• Life cycle of project teams<br>• Managing key stakeholders of projects<br>• Leading and motivating project team | |

# TABLES AND FORMULAE

Information concerning formulae and tables will be provided via the AICPA & CIMA website, www.aicpa-cima.com.

Section 1

# OBJECTIVE TEST QUESTIONS

## BUSINESS MODELS AND VALUE CREATION

**1 Cultural or demographic factors would generally be considered under which heading in the PEST(LE) framework?**

A Political

B Economic

C Social

D Technological

**2** WXY runs a chain of bars and night clubs within country H. It is considering extending its operations to neighbouring countries.

**Match up the following macro-economic factors with the heading they would be analysed under in a PESTLE analysis.**

| Political | Economic | Social | Technological | Legal | Environmental |
|---|---|---|---|---|---|

| |
|---|
| The age at which people are allowed to drink alcohol |
| Government tax on sales of alcohol |
| The level of disposable income people have |
| People's religious beliefs and attitudes towards alcohol |

**3** Ken is a successful entrepreneur. He is considering entering a new market which Ken considers will generate profits of over $30,000 per annum. Ken has discovered that to set up the new business he would have to purchase a machine costing $18,000, purchase a licence costing $3,000 and attend an intensive two-day training course.

**Which of the following situations would Porter's five forces model suggest?**

A The power of the supplier is low

B Rivalry is high

C The threat of new entrants is high

D The power of buyers is low

**4** PQR manufactures cardboard packaging. It is considering moving into the plastic packaging market. It has established that there are four main plastic packaging manufacturers, who have an aggregate market share of 82%. The current market leader has a share of 26%. The four companies produce products of similar size and quality. The market for plastic packaging has grown by 2% per annum in recent years.

**Complete the following sentence, identifying which aspect of Porter's five forces would consider this information and identify if the scenario suggests that the force would be high or low.**

| **Force** |
|---|
| New entrants |
| Power of buyers |
| Power of suppliers |
| Substitutes |
| Rivalry amongst competitors |

| **Strength** |
|---|
| Low |
| High |

The force which would consider this information is ____________ and from the scenario, the force would be ___________.

**5** **In Porter's five forces model, which of the following is NOT a barrier to entry for a new entrant to an industry?**

A Economies of scale exist

B Switching costs exist

C Numerous suppliers

D Product differentiation by existing participants

**6** Porter's work on industry competition suggests that the strength of market entry depends on the existence of barriers to entry.

**Identify THREE factors that create barriers to entering an industry.**

A Economies of scale

B Patents are required

C Expanding market

D Vertical integration

E Many small competitors

F Low capital requirements

**7** **As part of a Porter's 5 Forces analysis, which of the following would cause rivalry amongst existing competitors to be higher?**

A Rapid growth in the market

B High fixed costs

C Relative quality and costs of similar products

D High barriers to entry

**8** XYZ offers accountancy training courses. The market is growing quickly and XYZ's courses are significantly different to those offered by its rivals. Any new company wishing to teach accountancy courses must obtain accreditation by the various accountancy organisations. This process can take several years.

**Based on the above information, which of the following statements can be made about XYZ's competitive environment?**

A Competitive rivalry is likely to be low

B Supplier power is likely to be low

C Barriers to entry are likely to be low

D The threat of new entrants is likely to be low

**9** **According to Porter's five forces model, which of the following would tend to indicate there is a low threat of new entrants to the market?**

A Low capital requirements

B Patents exist on major product lines

C Access to distribution channels is not restricted

D Rapidly expanding market

**10** EFG sells motor vehicles in country V. It has recently discovered that the government is planning a major overhaul of the public transport system in V, which will significantly increase its speed and comfort, while lowering the cost to make it more attractive.

**Under which heading of Porter's five forces model would this issue be included?**

A Barriers to entry

B Power of suppliers

C Threat of substitutes

D Power of buyers

**11** **According to Porter, what are the three generic strategies through which an organisation can gain competitive advantage?**

A Cost leadership, Differentiation, Focus

B Market Penetration, Diversification, Product Development

C Internal development, Strategic alliances, Takeovers and mergers

D Corporate, Business, Operational

**12 Which of the following statements relating to big data is true?**

A Big data refers to any financial data over $1 billion

B Three of the main defining characteristics of big data are Velocity, Volume and Variety

C The term big data is defined as 'data that comes from many sources'

D Big data contains mainly non-financial data

**13 How is the delivery of on-demand computing resources otherwise known?**

A Artificial Intelligence

B The Internet of Things

C Big data

D Cloud computing

**14 Machines working and reacting like human beings describes what?**

A Robotics

B Voice recognition

C Artificial intelligence and machine learning

D The 4th Industrial Revolution

**15 Which THREE of the following statements about a blockchain are true?**

A Blockchain is regarded as a solution to cyber security risk

B Records in the blockchain are publicly available

C Records in the blockchain are kept private to enhance security

D The verification of transactions is carried out by computers

E The verification of transaction is carried out by individuals

E An example of blockchain is cryptocurrency

**16** The IBM report 'The New Age of Ecosystems' suggested that new technologies are changing the nature of business environments and specified three characteristics of such new environments.

**Which THREE of the following characteristics of ecosystems were specified in this report?**

A Complex and loose

B Simple and intelligent

C Connected and open

D Rich and sophisticated

E Transparent and orchestrated

F Fast and scalable

**17** W is a singer and guitarist from Newlandia who has gained a massive online following after posting his songs on social media. His last song received over five million likes, so W has employed an agent and is now looking to arrange a world tour.

W's agent will speak to promoters, venues, festival organisers and caterers but, because of his fame, W is able to dictate many aspects of the forthcoming tour. These include insisting all food is vegan, that a barrel of W's favourite beer is shipped out from Newlandia to each venue and that all vans and taxis used for transfers between airports, hotels and gigs have a Newlandia flag painted on them.

**Examine the above information and identify which of the following components of a network or ecosystem is being described:**

A Role

B Reach

C Rules

D Connections

**18** J used to work for a major guitar amplifier manufacturer until he observed a trend in the music industry away from traditional amplifiers towards digital modelling systems. Fearing his long-term job future was in doubt, he decided to set up his own business. However, instead of embracing the new digital technologies, J decided that there was a still a market for completely individual, bespoke, traditional guitar amplifiers – effectively a market segment of one. J's customers – mainly professional musicians and lawyers – can specify every aspect of their amplifier from the wood, the type of pre-amp and power-amp circuits used, the speaker choice and even whether they want 'new old stock' valves made in the 1960s to be used as components.

J's business model depends on being able to pass the specification for each order to his network of suppliers via 'the cloud', so suppliers can respond immediately to source, modify or make components to order and send them to Jessie within 48 hours. As a result, J can assemble, test and deliver the unique amp within a week of receiving the order.

**Which of the following components of an ecosystem is being described as central to J's business model?**

A Capability

B Rules

C Connections

D Course

**Note:** The scenarios in Q17 and Q18 are longer than would typically be seen in the E2 exam. However, they serve as excellent practise for applying knowledge to a given scenario.

**19 Which of the following statements about the differences between traditional markets and current thinking concerning ecosystems is/are true?**

(i) Both traditional markets and ecosystems assume that entities act out of individual self-interest.

(ii) Ecosystems create more value, as a whole, than the sum of individual participants acting independently in a traditional market.

A Statement (i) only

B Statement (ii) only

C Neither of them

D Both of them

**20** Wimber and Co are a specialist deep-sea oil-drilling company with an unparalleled reputation for successful drilling in locations that are high risk, whether due to strong currents, geothermal activity or other geological complications.

The oil drilling industry is tightly regulated, with the need to acquire permits from governments and to abide by a wide range of environmental and safety legislation.

**Which ecosystem archetype is being described here?**

A Hornet's nest

B Lion's pride

C Shark tank

D Wolf pack

**21** In the future, every home, building, facility or appliance may be both a consumer and producer of energy. Homes, for example, will likely sell into the grid during off times, such as daytimes when typically no one is at home, but solar panels are active. During peak demand times, homes may be a net consumer of energy. The presence of a strong regulator will ensure that energy flows are measured, reserve energy is stored, and networks remain in good working order.

**Based on the ecosystem archetype being described here, what is the likely strategy of participants in the energy industry?**

A Flying with hornets

B Roaring with lions

C Jumping with sharks

D Dancing with wolves

**22** J is in the process of buying a briefcase, as she has a new job and wishes to appear professional on her first day at work. He has searched several different retailers' websites and has noticed that the same model of briefcase (from a manufacturer called 'Casewise') appears on most of them.

**Identify which of the following strategies to react to the evolution of customer demands is being pursued by Casewise.**

A Brand atomisation

B Design thinking

C Experiential pilots

D Prototyping

**23** Drivers.com is a website dedicated to obtaining trusted and independent reviews of new car models. The organisation behind the website takes great care to ensure that reviews are only posted by people who have purchased and/or driven the car model they are reviewing. Any reviews that do not meet strict criteria are removed during the moderation process and never posted to the website.

According to the World Economic Forum/Accenture analysis, there are several factors that drive customer demands in the digital era.

**Examine the above statement and select which of the following 'drivers of customer demand in the digital era' is being described.**

A Contextualised interactions

B Transparency

C Peer review

D Seamless experience

**24** D is a governor at a school and has recently attended a meeting with headmasters, local government officials, the Member of Parliament for education and representatives of an economic 'think tank'. The discussion centred on delivering value for money in schools and included a discussion of key stakeholders (pupils, parents, teachers, etc.) and their objectives.

**Which aspect of defining, creating, delivering and capturing value is being described here?**

A Define value

B Create value

C Deliver value

D Capture residual value

**25** According to Mendelow, the significance of each stakeholder group in an organisation depends on two factors: the power of the stakeholder and the level of interest of the stakeholder.

| | | Interest | |
|---|---|---|---|
| | | Low | High |
| Power | Low | I | II |
| | High | III | IV |

**What approach is recommended for dealing with stakeholders in quadrant III of the above matrix?**

A Develop strategies that are fully acceptable to the stakeholder

B Keep the stakeholder satisfied

C Keep the stakeholder informed

D Minimum effort

**26** ABC is considering introducing greater use of robotics and AI within production, which would involve making 200 of its 3,000 employees redundant. Only around 2% of ABC's workers are members of a union.

**Select the most appropriate management strategy for the employees and place it in the correct area of the Mendelow matrix.**

| | low | **Interest** high |
|---|---|---|
| **Power** low | | |
| high | | |

Keep informed

Keep satisfied

Key players

Minimal effort

**27** **According to Mendelow, which of the following strategies should be used to deal with stakeholders who have low power but high interest?**

A Keep informed

B Minimal effort

C Keep satisfied

D Key player

**28** The directors of T, a high street retailer, have just had an emergency board meeting. The company has been facing tough trading conditions, due mainly to the growth of online shopping, and has had severe cash flow problems over the last 6 months. As a result of this, payments have not been made to key suppliers, nor into the firm's pension scheme. Furthermore, it looks unlikely that a forthcoming dividend payment will be met. On top of this, a key supplier has served notice that they intend to start a winding-up order against the company for failing to pay its debts.

**Using the urgency/power/legitimacy model identify which stakeholder the directors should prioritise?**

A Shareholders

B Current employees

C Retired employees

D Key suppliers

**29** In the CIMA® business model the concept of capturing value is linked to three key issues – the cost model, the revenue model and the distribution of surplus (or sharing residual value).

**Which of the following statements about these issues is/are true?**

(i) The cost model is effectively a variation of standard costing, so only budgeted costs are considered.

(ii) Key decision-making bases for sharing residual value are: tax strategy, dividend policy, desired capital structure and investment opportunities.

A Statement (i) only

B Statement (ii) only

C Neither of them

D Both of them

**30** Customer segments can be based on geography, demography, lifestyle, behaviour and purchase journey. Segments must be meaningful, mutually exclusive, measurable (with quantified market share), substantial, stable and easy to understand.

**Which of the following is NOT a characteristic of customers within highly desirable segments?**

A Frequent shoppers

B Are happy to try new items and typically return a high proportion of goods bought

C Use social media to tell friends about their purchases

D Regularly respond to special offers and promotions

**31** Customer segments can be based on geography, demography, lifestyle, behaviour and purchase journey.

**Which THREE of the following are demographic approaches to segmentation?**

A Gender

B Where customers live

C Income

D Social values

E Marital status

F Previous purchase history

**32** Customers might start the buying process based on the recommendation of a friend, online product research, or an email or text message offer. They might then touch and feel the product in a retail store but ultimately buy it from the comfort of their home via a tablet or other device late at night.

**Which characteristic of delivering value is being described in the above statement?**

A Segments must be meaningful, measurable and substantial

B Revenue needs to be converted into cash as quickly as possible

C Channels must be simple and transparent

D Channels must be integrated, turning shopping into a seamless experience

**33** In the CIMA® business model the concept of capturing value is linked to three key issues – the cost model, the revenue model and the distribution of surplus (or sharing residual value).

**Which of the following is a key factor when establishing cost architecture within the cost model?**

A Efficiency of the processes

B Investment opportunities

C Dividend policy

D Collection policy (terms of trade)

**34** **Which of the following statements concerning value is true?**

A Value is just another word for profit

B Companies should only focus on the tangible aspects of value

C Value involves both short-term and long-term aspects

D Creating value is just about increasing shareholder wealth

**35** A value proposition is defined as 'a reason given by a seller for buying their particular product or service, based on the value it offers customers'.

**Which of the following statements about value propositions is/are true?**

(i) In the 'define/create/deliver/capture' value cycle, formulating a value proposition is part of the 'deliver' phase.

(ii) When creating value five key elements must connect and align to create value at an appropriate cost. These are partners, resources, processes, activities and outputs, where 'outputs' are products, services and experience, which aim to meet the customer value proposition.

A Statement (i) only

B Statement (ii) only

C Neither of them

D Both of them

**36** YourFuture is a web-based project that aims to help schools and teachers improve the quality of career guidance provision with the use of digital tools. Key elements include guidelines for teachers, a web portal for career guidance for students, a quality framework for careers guidance, a web map device that can show geographic information on job opportunities and internships, a career guidance app for students that enables them to access the portal from their mobile devices and an e-learning platform for teachers.

**Match the following attributes of YourFuture with the five key elements of creating value within an ecosystem.**

| **Element** | **YourFuture** |
|---|---|
| Partners | YourFuture has designed a system where potential employers can populate information directly into the web portal. |
| Resources | The e-learning platform for teachers. |
| Processes | YourFuture uses its relationships with various employers to source the information needed for the web portal. |
| Activities | YourFuture's ecosystem includes university departments, local authorities, map providers and businesses. |
| Outputs | YourFuture uses a workflow system to allocate tasks and for operational reporting. |

**37** Firms can use a wide range of 'digital strategies' in order to overcome digital disruption and build disruptive and resilient business models.

**Drag and drop the following examples of digital strategies to align it with the correct category.**

| Category |
|---|
| Cryptocurrency |
| Platform |
| Fintech |
| IoT (Internet of Things) |

| Strategy |
|---|
| SwitchITon provides customers with a device and app that interconnect all their domestic appliances and allow them to be controlled remotely. |
| Car manufacturers that are members of DriveIT are sharing data collected from car operating systems with one-another, to improve the ways that all their vehicles operate and promote the sale of car-related products and services. |
| Buyers of gaming supplies (headsets, controllers, chairs etc.) from a range of retail websites can pay for those supplies using 'Creds', earned by winning online multi-player games. |
| PlaceIT is a portfolio management platform – taking business away from typically person-to-person advisers. Subscribers can use a smartphone app to get advice and manage their investment portfolio. |

**38** ChargeBest provides advice on travelling by hybrid and electric vehicles through a downloadable smartphone app. Users can input details of their vehicle and journey, and the app helps them to plan the route, and their re-charging stops according to the user's vehicle, preferences and favourite coffee shops.

The consultancy group Accenture wrote a report called Accenture Technology Vision, which highlighted five emerging trends that were shaping the digital landscape for organisations and which business leaders should focus on in developing digital strategies.

**Examine the above description and identify which of the trends identified by Accenture is being demonstrated by ChargeBest.**

A Workforce reimagined

B The intelligent enterprise

C The Internet of Me

D The platform (r)evolution

**39** ChargeBest provides advice on travelling by hybrid and electric vehicles. Users of ChargeBest's system can plan their route and their re-charging stops. To do this, ChargeBest gathers data from several partner organisations, including a digital mapping company, recharging equipment suppliers, and traffic information providers. This is updated, during the journey, by gathering GPS location data from the customer's smartphone.

The consultancy group Accenture wrote a report called Accenture Technology Vision, which highlighted five emerging trends that were shaping the digital landscape for organisations and which business leaders should focus on in developing digital strategies.

**Examine the above description and identify which of the trends identified by Accenture is being demonstrated by ChargeBest.**

A The outcome economy

B The intelligent enterprise

C The Internet of Me

D The platform (r)evolution

**40** In order for an organisation to properly take advantage of a move to digital, or to survive digital disruption within its industry, the executive leadership team will need to demonstrate eight key abilities. Some of those abilities focus on internal processes, while others are driven by the external business environment.

**Identify which of the leadership team abilities focus on external processes.**

A Inspirational leadership

B Competitive edge

C Establishing a strategic direction

D Collaboration

**41** Hannah is Non-Executive Chair of Balmer, a major provider of business broadband services. At a recent Board meeting of Balmer, Hannah urged the Board to shorten the company's planning horizon and to adopt a much more 'emergent' approach, to respond to increased rivalry and the rapid pace of technological change in Balmer's industry.

For an organisation to properly take advantage of a move to digital, or to survive digital disruption within its industry, the executive leadership team will need to demonstrate several abilities.

**Examine the description above and identify which of those abilities is being demonstrated by Hannah.**

A Establishing a strategic direction

B Business judgement

C Competitive edge

D Inspirational leadership

**42** Cate is a Non-Executive Director of King Tubby, and Chair of its Risk Committee. The Committee is currently examining a major proposed investment in 'cloud and mobile' technologies.

Cate has expressed the view that the cost of capital used in the investment appraisal is too high and, as a result, the project appears to add little shareholder value. Lori, the CFO of King Tubby, has advised that the cost of capital is high because King Tubby's bank has offered new debt finance (which is required for the project) at a much higher interest rate than previously.

Cate has offered to speak to the Lending Manager at King Tubby's bank, to persuade him of the strategic benefits of the cloud and mobile technologies. She hopes to persuade him to reduce the interest rate he has offered.

In order for an organisation to properly take advantage of a move to digital, or to survive digital disruption within its industry, the executive leadership team will need to demonstrate a number of abilities.

**Examine the description above and identify which of those abilities is being demonstrated by Cate.**

A Inspirational leadership

B Business judgement

C Influence external parties

D Collaboration

**43** Moss is a newspaper and magazine publisher. In 2000, all of Moss's publications were on paper. Over the subsequent 20 years, Moss changed its organisation structure, gathered all its digital talent together in one 'corporate lab', closed or sold nearly half of its titles, and migrated the rest (plus five new titles) onto digital platforms.

Research at the World Economic Forum on 'Digital Transformation of Industries' suggests that companies need to adopt one of (or a combination of) build, buy, partner, invest and incubate/accelerate if they wish to identify, develop and launch new business ventures.

**Identify which of these is being pursued by Moss.**

A Buy

B Build

C Invest

D Partner

**44** Charlie's is a successful chain of burger restaurants. It was formed in 1968 and, for forty years followed the conventional strategy of reinvesting profits into organic growth and franchising. By 2010, Charlie's was one of the largest fast-food chains in its home country and was considering its international growth options. To mitigate the risks of global expansion, Charlie's decided to enter into a strategic alliance with HomeServe, a global Internet-based food delivery platform. Knowing that it is possible to open a new restaurant and immediately serve customers who choose not to visit in person has so far allowed Charlie's to expand its network to over one thousand restaurants in eight countries.

Research at the World Economic Forum on 'Digital Transformation of Industries' suggests that companies need to adopt one of (or a combination of) build, buy, partner, invest and incubate/accelerate if they wish to identify, develop and launch new business ventures.

**Identify which of these is currently being pursued by Charlie's.**

A Partner

B Incubate/accelerate

C Invest

D Buy

**45** S retired at the age of 32 after a very successful career in football and decided to begin a second career. Sandy formed an equity investment trust with a friend, N, who advised wealthy sports stars how to invest their wealth. Together, the two began to acquire controlling stakes in small sports-related start-up businesses. Their investments helped these businesses to grow and, though not all the investments paid off, S and N now own significant stakes in over two hundred successful businesses despite not taking a management role in any of them. Most of these businesses use new technologies to deliver innovative and valuable packages of products and services to sports fans.

Research at the World Economic Forum on 'Digital Transformation of Industries' suggests that companies need to adopt one of (or a combination of) build, buy, partner, invest and incubate/accelerate if they wish to identify, develop and launch new business ventures.

**Identify which of these is being pursued by S and N.**

A Partner

B Build

C Incubate/accelerate

D Invest

**46** Ciao Bella is a major couture fashion brand. It was formed in 2007 by Bella McFarlane, a former model. Rather than design and manufacture its own garments, Ciao Bella has developed close relationships with many small fashion design companies and manufacturers. These small organisations were often start-up businesses, and sometimes just talented individuals. All the garments produced carry the Ciao Bella brand, together with the name of the designer and/or manufacturer. Ciao Bella garments are retailed online, and through major fashion retail chains. When a suitable partner organisation or individual has been identified, Ciao Bella provides development finance in return for shares, or provides loan capital. As part of the deal, Ciao Bella provides industry knowledge and access to technologies and logistics systems. More than three hundred organisations are now part of the Ciao Bella network.

Research at the World Economic Forum on 'Digital Transformation of Industries' suggests that companies need to adopt one of (or a combination of) build, buy, partner, invest and incubate/accelerate if they wish to identify, develop and launch new business ventures.

**Identify which of these is being pursued by Ciao Bella.**

A Partner

B Incubate/accelerate

C Build

D Invest

**47** The World Economic Forum project on the Digital Transformation of Industries (DTI) identified five successful digital operating models. They replace rigid approaches to technology, data and processes with flexibility, while also encouraging a culture that is open to innovation and interaction with customers and partners.

**Identify which THREE of the following are among the five DTI models.**

A Cost leadership

B Data-powered

C Market development

D Skynet

E Open and liquid

F Build

**48** Knife is an online retail platform for second-hand (used) books, toys and collectables. It links sellers with buyers and takes a small sales commission. Using sophisticated analytics and artificial intelligence applications, Knife can identify which of the books offered for sale is likely to appeal to which of its customers. Knife's sales application is therefore able to 'push' that book to the customers who are most likely to be interested in purchasing. Knife has very few permanent staff, but they are actively encouraged to innovate and to try out crazy ideas. As a result, Knife's offering is continually evolving.

The World Economic Forum project on the Digital Transformation of Industries (DTI) identified five successful digital operating models.

**Examine the above description and identify which of the DTI operating models is being used by Knife.**

A Data-powered

B Extra-frugal

C Skynet

D Customer-centric

**49** Orbital is a leading developer and producer of driverless vehicles. Since its foundation, in 2016, Orbital has developed three car models, two small delivery vans, a large lorry and an urban tram. Orbital was founded by three engineers and has a very strong culture of engineering excellence. Orbital has partnered with Sinkane, a manufacturer of industrial robots, to develop radically different ways of automating vehicle production. In return, Sinkane has agreed not to sell those robotic production technologies to other vehicle manufacturers for at least five years.

The World Economic Forum project on the Digital Transformation of Industries (DTI) identified five successful digital operating models.

**Examine the above description and identify which of the DTI operating models is being used by Orbital.**

A Data-powered

B Extra-frugal

C Skynet

D Customer-centric

**50** The World Economic Forum on the Digital Transformation of Industries identified five successful digital operating models. They replace rigid approaches to technology, data and processes with flexibility, while also encouraging a culture that is open to innovation and interaction with customers and partners.

**Drag and drop the following descriptions to align each with the appropriate operating model.**

| Operating model |
|---|
| Customer-centric |
| Extra-frugal |
| Data-powered |
| Skynet |
| Open and liquid |

| Description |
|---|
| This model looks outward with a view to creating an ecosystem that can enrich the customer proposition. Built around a sharing customer, all processes are characterised by a constant flow of dialogue with the outside world. |
| This model is built around prowess in analytics and software intelligence. Data-powered companies have an agile culture focused on innovation through empirical experimentation. |
| This model focuses on making customers' lives easier and emphasises front-office processes. It works best with a culture that puts the client first and a decentralised structure that empowers frontline staff. |
| This model makes intensive use of machines to increase productivity and flexibility in production. Skynet organisations are characterised by an engineer-led culture dedicated to automation. |
| This model thrives on a culture of 'less is more' and a standardised organisational structure. By optimising manufacturing, supply and support processes, it can provide a high-quality service at a low cost. |

**51** Lizzo has established a 'new employee referral programme', where existing employees are rewarded for proposing a friend or contact for a role at Lizzo. In this way, Lizzo spends very little on recruitment, while widening its pool of skilled staff, and existing employees receive a substantial bonus when their referral is hired.

The World Economic Forum Digital Transformation of Industries project (DTI) proposed a 7-step process to build a 'digital workforce'.

**Examine the above description and identify which of the steps proposed by the DTI is being described.**

A Integrate your on-demand workforce

B Bring leadership into the digital age

C Attract and retain talent

D Foster a digital culture in the enterprise

**52** KTJ is a traditional high-street furniture retailer. As part of its 'going digital' strategy, KTJ has just created the post of 'Digital Visionary' on its Board and recruited a senior manager from a social media company to fill the vacancy.

The World Economic Forum Digital Transformation of Industries project (DTI) proposed a 7-step process to build a 'digital workforce'.

**Examine the above description and identify which of the steps proposed by the DTI is being described.**

A Become an employer of choice for the latest generation of employees

B Create a workforce with digital skills

C Foster a digital culture in the enterprise

D Attract and retain talent

**53** L Company is looking at various options to implement its new 'Digital Vision'. One of the options, which L has chosen, is to create a business incubator to allow staff to develop new technological ideas into viable internal processes or commercial propositions.

The World Economic Forum Digital Transformation of Industries project (DTI) proposed a 7-step process to build a 'digital workforce'.

**Examine the above description and identify which of the steps proposed by the DTI is being described.**

A Become an employer of choice for the latest generation of employees

B Attract and retain talent

C Bring leadership into the digital age

D Foster a digital culture in the enterprise

**54** **Which of the following statements about bringing leadership to the digital age is/are true?**

(i) Firms need to develop a culture that is more risk-tolerant and accepts failure.

(ii) Firms need to use more short-term goals and targets in order to keep control of the business.

A Statement (i) only

B Statement (ii) only

C Neither of them

D Both of them

**55** Charlton Company is a major manufacturer of ground-source heat-pumps. These devices allow users to extract geothermal energy from the earth, and to use that energy to heat their premises. In order to develop new products and services, Charlton has already developed mutually beneficial relationships with its supply chain and key customers.

Charlton Inc is currently analysing its business environment and has realised that there might be competitive advantage to be gained by treating its environment as an 'ecosystem'. This is not something that has ever been done in Charlton's industry.

**Align each of the following 'competitive forces' to match the likely effect of Charlton's new approach. You may use each effect more than once.**

| Force |
|---|
| Bargaining power of suppliers |
| Bargaining power of customers |
| Competitive rivalry |
| Threat of new entrants |

| Effect |
|---|
| Increase |
| Decrease |
| Remain stable |
| |

**56** Geronimo is a consumer electronics manufacturer. It produces hardware communications devices (tablets, laptops, PCs and phones) and supplies a range of software to operate on those devices (operating systems, tools and apps).

Geronimo has developed a close working relationship, for mutual benefit, with a network of other organisations and individuals. These include software developers, suppliers, retailers and consumers. As a result of these arrangements, Geronimo and its partners create and capture value added, which is shared between the partners.

**Identify which of the following approaches is being taken by Geronimo.**

A Franchising

B Ecosystem development

C Upstream supply chain management

D Customer relationship management

**57** The Competition and Markets Regulator (CMR) of Newlandia is tasked with regulating the activities of firms within that country. The regulators are finding it increasingly difficult to regulate the activities of organisations who choose to participate in a 'business ecosystem'.

**Identify which THREE of the following are major challenges to the CMR as a result of firms taking an ecosystem approach.**

A New legislation is expensive to develop

B Speed of change

C Data protection is a major issue

D Ecosystems evolve

E Innovations cross lines of jurisdiction

F Customers are demanding a more personalised experience

**58 Which THREE of the following are consequences of the developments in mobile technologies?**

A The decline of the newspaper industry

B The decline of social media interactions

C A decline in high street banking

D An increase in the on-demand nature of music

E An increase in the cost to manufacture smart devices

F Connectivity with customers is slower

**59** Trusted traders are a new business comprising a franchised network of trades people such as plumbers, electricians, builders and carpenters. Each franchisee has an app that enables them to log and record the expenses they incur as well as scanning all receipts for materials purchased.

**What type of technology are they making use of?**

A Social media

B Internet of things

C An intranet

D Mobile technology

**60 Images, audio files and animations are all examples of what?**

A Technology

B Big data

C Information

D Digital assets

# MANAGING PEOPLE PERFORMANCE

**61 Which THREE of the following are advantages to an individual of a performance appraisal system?**

A Feedback about performance and assessment of competence

B Provides a basis for remuneration

C It provides clear targets linked to corporate objectives

D Provides a basis for HR planning

E Helps control salary costs

F Identifies training and development needs

**62** Q recently attended a management training course where she learnt about the 360 approach to performance appraisal. Q's company has grown significantly in the past few years, and she is keen to introduce such a system.

**Which of the following is an advantage of using the 360 approach?**

A It focuses on pre-agreed targets

B It encourages individuals to work together for the good of the department

C It aims to capture all aspects of performance

D It requires the subordinate to appraise their own performance

**63** X is trying to communicate with all the staff within the department. X has placed the information on the business intranet, but after a week very few staff members have seen the information. X has been told by several colleagues that they 'never really look on the intranet' and so they had failed to see X's message.

**Which aspect of the communication process has caused this problem?**

A X's communication has suffered from too much noise

B X has encoded the message poorly

C X has chosen the wrong channel

D X's communication has not been accurately decoded

**64** Four members of staff in a department came back to work an hour late from lunch:

Employee 1 has had 2 written warnings about lateness.

Employee 2 has just started work with the company a few days ago.

Employee 3 has already had an informal chat regarding this issue.

Employee 4 has recently returned from a period of suspension for excessive lateness.

**What would be the most appropriate next stage of action for each of these employees as part of a disciplinary process?**

| |
|---|
| An oral warning |
| Dismissal, demotion or transfer |
| An informal talk |
| Suspension without pay |

**65** Below are four short descriptions of leadership and management theories:

- There is one best way to undertake every task.
- Interpersonal relations are a key part of determining workplace behaviour.
- Managers must control the needs of the task, individual and group.
- Managers can be either a psychologically distant or psychologically close.

**Match the descriptions above to the correct theory from the following list:**

- **Adair's action-centred leadership**
- **Human relations school**
- **McGregor's Theory X and Theory Y**
- **Fiedler's contingency theory**
- **Taylor's scientific management**
- **Blake and Mouton's managerial grid**

**66** In Drucker's Management by Objectives model, he suggests that organisations require multiple objectives.

**Which of the following are THREE of Drucker's key objectives?**

A Innovation

B Public responsibility

C Employee satisfaction

D Sales revenue

E Productivity

F Market share

**67** **Which of the following is NOT an advantage of an effective performance appraisal system?**

A Improves communication between managers and subordinates

B Helps identify training needs

C Ensures performance targets are met

D Provides a fair process for reward decisions

**68** Consider the following benefits:

(i) Reduced training costs within the organisation

(ii) Better local decisions due to local expertise

(iii) Better motivation of staff

(iv) Reduction in suboptimal behaviour

**Which of these are advantages of the personal centralised control of decision-making within an organisation?**

A (i) and (ii) only

B (i), (ii) and (iii) only

C (iii) only

D (i) and (iv) only

**69 Which TWO of the following are responsible for an employee's health and safety in the workplace?**

(1) The employer

(2) The internal auditor

(3) The employee

(4) The health and safety advisor

A (1) and (2)

B (1) and (3)

C (3) and (4)

D (2) and (3)

**70 Intrinsic satisfaction is said to be derived from which of the following?**

A Perks of the job

B Job content

C Job rewards

D Group cohesiveness and belonging

**71 What type of power is a manager using when they promote a member of staff on merit?**

A Referent

B Expert

C Coercive

D Reward

**72 In the Blake and Mouton managerial grid, shown below, match the styles to the correct place on the grid.**

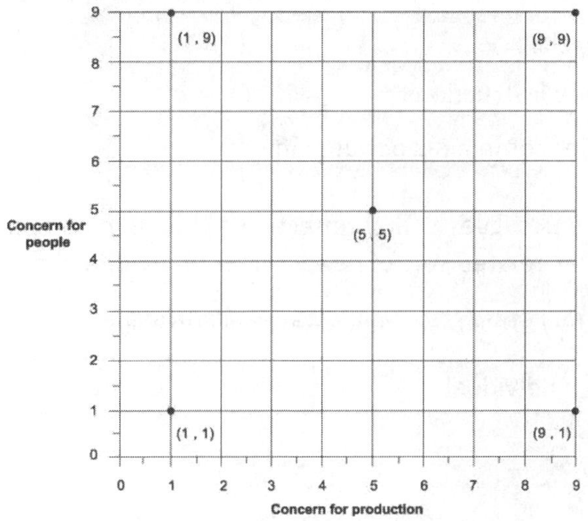


| |
|---|
| Task orientated |
| Country-club |
| Impoverished |
| Team style |
| Middle road |

**73** According to Herzberg's motivation theory, factors can be hygiene factors or motivators.

**Match the following as to whether they relate to hygiene factors or motivators:**

- These help to avoid unpleasantness and dissatisfaction
- Good working conditions
- An appropriate level of salary
- Career advancement
- These satisfy the need for personal growth

**74** Dismissal would occur at final stage in disciplinary action is dismissal. Prior to this, several other steps should be followed:

1 Oral warning

2 Informal talk

3 Suspension

4 Final written warning

5 First written warning

**List the numbers in the order in which the stages would occur in a disciplinary procedure:**

A 2, 1, 3, 5, 4

B 1, 5, 2, 4, 3

C 2, 1, 5, 4, 3

D 2, 1, 3, 4, 5

**75 Which of the following statements is an advantage of a good grievance procedure?**

A It ensures the legal obligations of the employer are met

B It reduces employee morale and trust

C It ensures all employees will follow instructions

D It reduces the number of customer complaints about staff

**76** Adair's action-centred leadership model suggests that effective leadership depends on balancing the priority given to three inter-related sets of needs – task, individual and group.

Match the following roles to whether they are a task, individual or group roles.

| Task | Individual | Group |
|---|---|---|

- Opinion-seeking
- Employee feedback
- Peace keeping
- Communicating
- Decision making
- Employee counselling

**77** Within the organisational iceberg, some items are defined as visible and others as hidden.

**Which THREE of the following would be defined as visible elements?**

A Attitudes

B Goals

C Style

D Values

E Skills

F Technology

**78** The following assumptions underlie a well-known theory of motivation.

The expenditure of physical and mental effort at work is as natural as play or rest.

If a job is satisfying, then the result will be commitment to the organisation.

**These assumptions apply to which of the following models?**

A Maslow's hierarchy of needs

B McGregor's Theory X

C McGregor's Theory Y

D Hertzberg's motivation theory

**79** **Which approach to control is likely to be found in small owner-managed organisations where there is centralised decision-making by the owner?**

A Personal centralised control

B Output control

C Clan or Cultural control

D Bureaucratic control

**80** **Which of the following statements relating to Health and Safety in the workplace is NOT true?**

A Managing health and safety in the workplace is a legal requirement

B Health and safety controls can save companies money

C Managing health and safety is solely the responsibility of directors

D Provision of training for employees is part of health and safety requirements

**81** Equal opportunities and diversity in the workplace are often confused.

**Match the following to whether they relate to diversity or equal opportunities?**

- Its purpose is to remove discrimination
- It relies on proactive action
- It is a Human Resources role
- It is a managerial role

**82** **Adair's action-centred leadership model is part of which of the following schools of thought?**

A Human relations school

B Classical school

C Contingency school

D Scientific school

**83** H is a new employee at JHI. O, a long-serving employee, has been asked to offer H any practical advice and support that she needs and act as a role model for H.

**O would therefore be classified as H's:**

A Coach

B Mentor

C Counsellor

D Partner

**84 Which THREE of the following statements regarding authority and responsibility are true?**

A Authority is the right to exercise power

B Traditional authority is based on Weber's classical bureaucracy

C Responsibility is the capacity to exert influence

D When delegating, responsibility can never be delegated

E Responsibility requires individuals to explain and justify any failure to fulfil their responsibilities to their superiors

F Responsibility means the right to hold subordinates accountable for their performance and achievements

**85** The Finance Director of CDE Company is dismissed without notice. Their contract of employment gives an entitlement to one year's notice of termination of employment. Under UK law, the director could bring an action for ________ or ________ dismissal.

**Which of the following words most accurately fill the gaps?**

| | | | | |
|---|---|---|---|---|
| Redundancy | Termination | Dismissal without notice | Negligence | Unfair |

**86** AJ Co manufactures motorbikes.

**Which of the following statements is consistent with Taylor's theory of scientific management?**

A AJ should create employee suggestion schemes to generate ideas for how to improve its operations

B AJ should focus on improving group relations and team spirit within its workforce

C AJ does not need to set detailed standards for hiring workers as it should provide detailed training for all new employees

D AJ's managers should make all key decisions and provide detailed instructions to workers

**87** J is a manager with EFG Company. She does not get on well with the employees who report to her and has little real power to punish or reward the staff for their behaviour.

**Which of the following management styles does Fiedler suggest would work best for J?**

A Psychologically close

B Psychologically open

C Psychologically committed

D Psychologically distant

**88** **Which of these steps aimed at increasing job satisfaction could be attributed to the findings of the human relation school?**

A Creating an open-office environment so people can socialise more freely

B Paying staff for each hour worked or item produced

C Managers setting challenging individual targets

D Producing an organisational chart, so staff are aware of where they stand in the hierarchy

**89** EFG is a large organisation with a range of incentives available to motivate and improve the performance of its staff.

**Which of the following incentives will be most appropriate for staff working in the HR department?**

A Commission

B Piece rate

C Profit sharing

D Productivity plans

**90** A manager is planning on introducing a new computer system into her department. She plans to offer her staff bonuses to encourage them to use the new system, as well as relying on her own personal charisma.

**Which THREE of the following sources of power is the manager planning to use?**

A Reward

B Legitimate

C Referent

D Coercive

E Expert

F Autocratic

**91** The Equality Act 2010 aims to strengthen the protection against discrimination in the workplace and in the wider society. According to the act, it is unlawful to discriminate against people on a number of grounds.

**Which of the following grounds for discrimination is NOT covered by the act?**

A Marriage and civil partnership

B Religion or belief

C Physical appearance

D Age

**92 Which of the following is NOT a requirement of effective delegation?**

A Clearly defining the subordinate's goals and the limits of the delegated authority

B Ensuring that the subordinate will be able to undertake the task competently

C Backing off so that the subordinate must perform the task unassisted

D Reviewing results and offering feedback on performance at agreed points

**93 Which THREE of the following would be a justified reason for redundancy?**

A Where an employee's conduct is unacceptable

B Where a department or team persistently underperforms

C Where an employee is no longer legally able to perform the role

D Where the type of work which the employee undertakes is no longer carried out

E Where an employee's part of the business ceases trading

F The business ceases trading

**94 In a typical hierarchical organisation, the requirement of a lower-level manager to answer to a higher-level manager in the chain of command is referred to as:**

A authority

B empowerment

C accountability

D super-ordination

**95 At which level of control within an organisation would the setting of the control environment be a responsibility?**

A Strategic

B Operational

C Tactical

D Group

**96** According to Schein, culture exist at three levels: 'Artefacts', 'Values' and 'Basic assumptions'.

**Which THREE of the following relate to Values?**

A The things that can be seen, heard and observed

B Deeply held beliefs

C The things that can be identified from stories

D The way we do things around here

E How people justify what they do

F The behaviour people feel is important

**97 Which of the following is seen as a disadvantage of having a strong culture?**

A Strong cultures may regulate behaviour and norms within the organisation

B Strong cultures may reduce differences amongst the members of the organisation

C Strong cultures may affect the organisation's ability or desire to learn new skills

D Strong cultures may facilitate good communication and coordination within the organisation

**98 Which contemporary writer argued that we need to be able view organisations from a range of different perspectives in order to understand and improve effectiveness and that three key perspectives were organisations as machines, organisations as organisms and organisations as cultures?**

A Adair and Fiedler

B Morgan

C Burns and Stalker

D Trist and Bamforth

**99 Which THREE of the following statements regarding management concepts are correct?**

A Responsibility can be delegated but authority cannot

B Authority can be delegated but responsibility cannot

C The scope of responsibility must always exceed the scope of authority

D Traditional authority is based on custom and practice

E Power is the ability to exert influence

F Delegation is where employees are given autonomy and responsibility to undertake tasks without being directed at each step by management

**100 In the context of a balanced scorecard approach to the provision of management information, which THREE of the following measures might be appropriate for monitoring the innovation and learning perspective?**

A Training days per employee

B Employee satisfaction

C Cost income ratio

D Percentage of revenue generated by new products or services

E Customer satisfaction

F Number of new product design ideas per employee

**101** G is a member of a project team. Colleagues in the team rely on him to read and check complex project documentation. G has a keen eye for detail and often identifies minor details in documents that others miss but may be of significance. Despite this diligent approach, G always meets his deadlines. However, Some of G's colleagues feel frustrated when he refuses to involve others. G can hold up progress as he will not agree to the team signing off project documents until all of G's concerns are fully discussed.

**According to Belbin's team roles theory, G is an example of which of the following?**

A Implementer

B Completer-finisher

C Monitor-evaluator

D Shaper

**102 Match the types of conflict to the correct statement:**

| | |
|---|---|
| Horizontal | Tends to cause alienation between groups and individuals |
| Vertical | Considered positive and beneficial to the organisation |
| Constructive | Occurs between departments at the same level in the organisation |
| Destructive | Occurs between individuals and groups at different levels |

**103** J manages a team of workers within his department. He has recently sat in on a team meeting during which the team had started discussing which roles each team member would take on.

**Which of Tuckman's stages of group development does J's team appear to have reached?**

A Storming

B Norming

C Performing

D Forming

**104 Contingency theorists believe that:**

A effective management is primarily a function of successful people management

B organisational achievement is largely contingent upon general economic circumstances

C major change is dependent primarily upon clarity and communication of the strategic vision

D lessons of earlier theorists should be adapted to suit circumstances

**105** Belbin suggested a number of team roles including the following:

| | | | | |
|---|---|---|---|---|
| Team worker | Plant | Monitor-Evaluator | Completer Finisher | Implementer (company worker) |

**Match the following personalities to the appropriate role defined by Belbin.**

A S is a very quiet person, she often reserves her opinion until being directly asked for it however she always offers unusual and creative suggestions when the team is faced with difficult problem

B J is respected by all team members for high quality analytical skills, though he rarely gets invited to out-of-office private parties as many find J tactless

C E is the company's HR manager, she ensures that any potential conflicts are promptly identified and resolved, and the team members work harmoniously

**106 Which of the following LEAST accurately completes the statement: 'A win-win negotiation strategy is most likely when...'**

A both parties are aggressive

B both parties focus on problem-solving strategies

C both parties adopt a collaborative approach

D both parties are assertive

**107** EFG has a large marketing department.

**In which THREE of the following ways would this department co-ordinate with EFG's finance department?**

A Decisions on the quantity of raw materials required

B Establishing credit terms for customers

C Budgeting for sales volumes

D Calculating pay rises for staff

E Decisions on the selling price of the product

F Determining market share

**108 Which of the following statements is correct with regards to the differences between individuals and teams?**

A Teams tend to enjoy synergies which cannot be achieved by individual workers

B Teams tend to make decisions more rapidly than individuals

C Individuals are less likely to make definite decisions and rely on compromises

D There are fewer controls in place when groups make decisions

**109** There are several techniques which can be used to manage inter-group conflict, including:

| | | | |
|---|---|---|---|
| Third party consultants | Member rotation | Superordinate goals | Confrontation |

**Match the following descriptions to the correct technique:**

- This technique involves the conflicting party directly engaging with each other and negotiating with one another to try to work out their differences.
- This technique involves management imposing shared targets on both parties which will require the cooperation of both parties in order to meet the target.
- With this technique, members of one department will be asked to work in the other department for a period of time, to allow them to better understand the issues faced by the other department.
- A technique which can be used where conflicting parties are uncooperative is to bring in an independent party to meet with the conflicting parties to encourage them to reach agreement.

**110 Which of the following can be used to describe the homogeneity of objectives and thinking in group work?**

A The Abilene Paradox

B Risky shift

C Group polarisation

D Groupthink

**111 The four steps to negotiating an agreement go in what order:**

A persuade other party, know the background, influence the other party, agreement is reached

B proposing a solution, clarifying objectives, narrow the gap, obtain feedback

C information gathering, present their starting positions, narrow the gap, agreement is reached

D information gathering, present their starting positions, look for a mutually beneficial outcome, narrow the gap

**112** Mainwaring suggested four conflict managing strategies:

| | | | |
|---|---|---|---|
| Stimulation and orchestration | Suppression | Reduction | Resolution |

**Match the strategy to the definitions given below:**

A Involves the use or threatened use of authority or force

B Seeks to eliminate the root causes of conflict

C Involves building on areas of agreement and on common objectives

D Actively encourages conflict as a means of generating new ideas and new approaches or of stimulating change

**113** According to Cialdini, when trying to influence another person, the following six principles of influence can be used:

- Reciprocity
- Commitment
- Social proof
- Liking
- Authority
- Scarcity

**Match the following actions taken to the correct principle:**

A Remind the person of things you have done for them in the past

B Advise people that they could lose out if they don't act quickly

C Use the opinions of those already supporting you to influence others to join that support

D Building relationships with the people you want to influence so that they trust you

**114** Consider the following two statements:

(1) According to Bennis, transactional leaders offer rewards to their followers in exchange for their compliance.

(2) Contingency theories of management suggest that certain leadership approaches can be learnt and used by managers.

**Which of these options is/are correct?**

A (1) only

B (2) only

C Both

D Neither

**115 Research on group effectiveness has concluded that the most consistently successful groups:**

A are those in which all members are innovative

B comprise a range of roles undertaken by various members

C are those in which all members are very intelligent

D comprise a range of roles all undertaken by a few members of the group

**116** Tuckman identified five stages in group development.

**In which order do the stages occur?**

A Forming, adjourning, storming, performing, norming

B Forming, norming, storming, performing, adjourning

C Storming, forming, performing, adjourning, norming

D Forming, storming, norming, performing, adjourning

**117** The finance function can be positioned in different ways within the organisation.

**Complete the following sentences relating to the types of groups in an organisation using the following:**

| | |
|---|---|
| Formal groups | Informal groups |
| Reference groups | Self-directed groups |

_________ are those the individual does not currently belong to but wants to join.

_________ are those in which membership is normally voluntary and informal.

_________ are created by the organisation to carry out specific tasks, communicate and solve problems.

_________ are encouraged to manage their own work and practices.

**118 The conflict management strategy recommended by the Thomas-Kilmann Conflict Mode Instrument as a means of finding a win:win situation is which of the following?**

A Compromising

B Competing

C Collaborating

D Accommodating

**119 Which of the following statements about non-verbal communication is NOT true?**

A Non-verbal action can vary across countries and cultures

B The actual words said are just as important as the way they are said

C Physical gestures such as a handshake or a pat on the back are considered non-verbal communication

D Appearance and posture are important elements of communication

**120 Negotiation is a process in which:**

A Two or more parties try to initiate differences

B Two or more parties try to avoid differences

C Two or more parties try to prevent differences

D Two or more parties try to resolve differences

**121 Match the different team roles, as defined by Belbin, to the following descriptions:**

| | |
|---|---|
| Plant | Supports other members of the team and helps to promote harmony. |
| Completer Finisher | Imaginative and very good at coming up with original ideas and suggestions. |
| Team Worker | Gives attention to detail and is concerned with meeting deadlines. |

**122 Which of the following is a strategy for managing conflict explained by Mainwaring?**

A Suppression

B Negotiation

C Discipline

D Persuasion

**123 What name did Tuckman give to the stage of team development in which the team responds well to the team leader, roles and responsibilities are clear and accepted, commitment is strong and major decisions are taken by group agreement?**

A Storming

B Performing

C Forming

D Norming

**124 Match the following statements with the level of Maslow's hierarchy of needs.**

(i) A has been offered a large pay rise in recognition of A's hard work on several recent projects.

(ii) B has been offered a permanent contract with the business she works for, giving her access to a good pension scheme.

(iii) C has been offered her first ever job with a company. The pay she receives will be sufficient to cover her essential costs.

A (i) – Basic, (ii) – Ego, (iii) – Security

B (i) – Self-fulfilment, (ii) – Basic, (iii) – Social

C (i) – Ego, (ii) – Security, (iii) – Basic

D (i) – Ego, (ii) – Social, (iii) – Security

**125 In Belbin's team roles, which role is defined as 'committed to the task, may be aggressive and challenging, will always promote activity'?**

A Shaper

B Plant

C Team Worker

D Completer Finisher

**126 Identify, in the correct order, the four main stages in the negotiation process.**

| | |
|---|---|
| 1 | Bargaining |
| 2 | Preparation |
| 3 | Closing |
| 4 | Opening |

**127 Vaill suggested that high performing teams had several common characteristics. Which THREE of the following are some of those characteristics?**

A Strong and clear leadership

B Commitment to purposes

C The team should be of limited duration

D The team should be small

E Generation of inventions and new methods

F Voluntary membership

**128 Which type of leadership is more horizontal in nature, rather than more vertical or hierarchical?**

A Autocratic

B Traditional

C Free rein

D Distributed

**129** Group working can bring many advantages, but it can also bring some problems.

**Match the problem with group working with its description:**

| Problem | Description |
|---|---|
| Conformity | Groups can end up taking decisions which are riskier than the individual members would take |
| Abilene paradox | Group members reach consensus without critically testing, analysing and evaluating ideas |
| Risky shift | The group can end up with an outcome which none of the members wanted |
| Groupthink | Individuals within the group can be persuaded to accept decisions which they know to be wrong |

**130** When working in groups, the combined activity of the group can be greater than the sum of the activities of each member of the group.

**What is the name given to this phenomenon?**

A Norming

B Groupthink

C Synergy

D Conformity

**131** Mainwaring suggested a number of causes of conflict including:

| |
|---|
| Interdependencies |
| Misunderstandings |
| Conviction beliefs |
| History |

**Complete the following sentences using some of the above words:**

Where boundaries between departments are not clearly defined, this can cause problems of __________.

Communication problems can lead to __________.

__________ suggests that conflict tends to be self-perpetuating.

**132** **Match the element of the communication process to its description.**

| | |
|---|---|
| What is being transmitted | Decoding |
| The medium through which the message is being sent | Feedback |
| The message is translated, and its meaning is generated | Channel |
| The receiver responds to the message | Noise |
| Anything which stops the message being transmitted as intended | Message |

**133** There are two types of conflict within an organisation:

| | |
|---|---|
| Horizontal | Vertical |

**Match the following statements to whether they relate to horizontal or vertical conflict.**

A Conflict occurring between groups and departments at the same level in the hierarchy.

B Where functional specialisms cause differences in cognitive and emotional orientations.

C A reward system based only departmental performance may encourage managers to meet goals at the expenses of other departments.

D Physiological distance can make workers feel isolated from the organisation.

**134** According to Cialdini, there are six principles of influence:

| |
|---|
| Reciprocity |
| Commitment |
| Social Proof |
| Liking |
| Authority |
| Scarcity |

**Match the following descriptions to the correct principle.**

A Identify what you want to achieve and what you need from the other person then consider what you may be able to offer them

B Build relationships with those you want to influence so that they trust you

C Use the opinions of those already supporting you to influence others to join that support

**135 Which of the following statements relating to non-verbal communication is NOT true?**

A Maintaining eye contact is an important element of non-verbal communication

B Non-verbal actions can help to ensure that the message is communicated correctly

C Non-verbal actions are universally understood

D The tone used when conversing is an important part of the communication process

**136 Complete the following sentences about teams using the correct theorist:**

| | | |
|---|---|---|
| Belbin | Tuckman | Vaill |

__________ suggested that teams typically pass through several stages of development.

__________ claimed that high-performance teams had several common characteristics.

__________ suggested that a well-balanced group should contain nine identified character types.

**137 Match the problems with meetings with the actions which could be taken to avoid them.**

| **Problem** | **Action** |
|---|---|
| Attendees talk too much | Ensure the correct attendees are invited |
| Objectives of the meeting are unclear | Ensure action points agreed, and minutes of meeting are issued |
| Action points from previous meetings not carried out | Agenda should be circulated before the meeting |
| Lack of enthusiasm at the meeting | Chairperson should impose order |

**138 Which of the following statements about persuasion is true?**

A Persuasion is a weaker form of influence

B Persuasion can be direct or indirect

C The six principles of influence can be used in persuasion

D In persuasion you are basically telling the other person what to do

**139** S, an employee, has resigned from their role as a machine operative because their employer failed to provide a safe and healthy working environment.

**Which of the following terms best describes this?**

A Wrongful dismissal

B Arbitration

C Constructive dismissal

D Collective grievance

**140 The strategy for managing conflict which involves building on areas of agreement and on common objectives, and changing attitudes and perceptions of the parties involved is known as which of the following?**

A Conflict stimulation and orchestration

B Conflict suppression

C Conflict reduction

D Conflict resolution

# MANAGING PROJECTS

**141 Which of the following is NOT a primary constraint?**

A Quality

B Time

C Cost

D Ethics

**142** A number of tools are used in planning for activities and costs within a project, including:

| |
|---|
| Work breakdown structure |
| Work packages and Statements of work |
| Product breakdown structure |
| Cost breakdown structure |

**Match the tool to its purpose from the following list.**

| |
|---|
| To specify the work to be done for each activity and who will carry it out |
| To cost each element of the project |
| To divide the work to be carried out into manageable pieces |
| To identify the product purchases required for each activity |

**143 Configuration management is designed to:**

A track deviation from proposed deliverables

B track deviation from schedule

C track product changes and versions

D track co-ordination between different project teams

**144 According to Gido and Clements, during which phase in the project lifecycle would a feasibility study be undertaken?**

A Identification of a need

B Development of a proposed solution

C Implementation

D Completion

**145 Which THREE of the following are reasons why a project would be initiated?**

A Process service enhancement

B Development of a proposed solution

C Statutory/legal requirement

D Performance enhancement

E Solve internal identified problems

F Eliminate project constraints

**146 Match the benefit to the project management tool.**

| | |
|---|---|
| Resource histogram | Establishes the authority and responsibility for each part of the project |
| Critical path analysis | Identifies the activities that cannot overrun without delaying the overall project completion |
| PERT | Allows a calculation of contingency to be added to the project plan |
| Breakdown structures | Helps with capacity planning |

**147 During the planning stage of a project, which THREE of the following might require separate detailed plans to be prepared?**

A Deliverables

B Stakeholders

C Chain of command

D Quality

E Contingency

F Scope

**148** GL is an inexperienced project manager who, on previous attempts at the role was criticised by the project sponsor for the lack of reporting throughout the project.

**Which THREE of the following are benefits of regular reporting throughout the duration of the project?**

A Comparison with planned performance

B Stakeholders can follow project progress

C Highlights any corrective action required

D Change control

E Risk management

F Eliminates deviations from the project plan

**149** In the PRINCE2 project organisational structure, a team that provides an independent view of how the project is progressing, reflecting business, user and specialist interests, is called a project __________team.

**Which of the following words correctly fills the gap in the above definition?**

A Steering

B Management

C Assurance

D Support

**150** The Project Management Institute's five process areas are:

A Executing

B Initiating

C Closing

D Controlling

E Planning

**Place the process area in the correct place in the following diagram:**

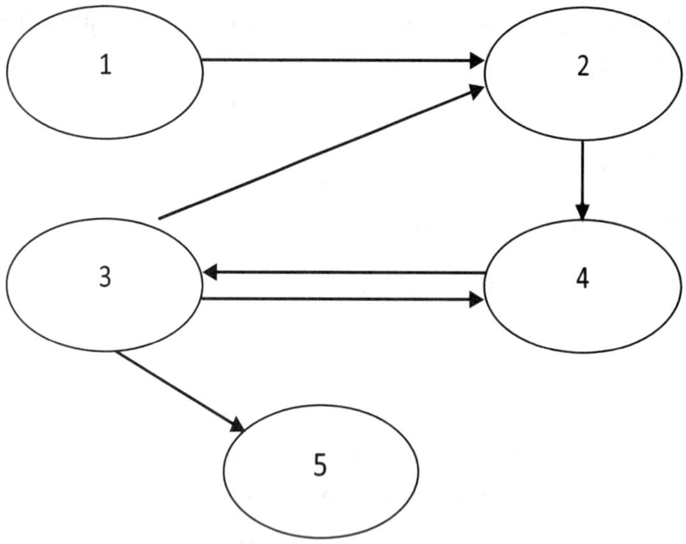


**151 Who is ultimately responsible for closing down an unsuccessful project?**

A Project team

B Project steering committee

C Project owner

D Project customer

**152 A hierarchical view of the way a project is structured, identifying progressively detailed task elements, is known as which of the following?**

A CBS

B CPA

C WBS

D PID

**153** There is some confusion in D Company as to responsibility of different project stakeholders in the management of projects.

**Which of the following project stakeholders is responsible for the scope and functionality of a project?**

A Project sponsor

B Project steering committee

C Project owner

D Project manager

**154** **The extent of work needed to produce the project's deliverables is known as which of the following?**

A Scale

B Cycle

C Time frame

D Scope

**155** A project manager requires a number of skills.

**Which of the following skills is NOT necessarily required by a project manager?**

A Leadership and delegation

B Change management and problem-solving

C Specialist financial

D Negotiation

**Questions 156, 157 and 158 are based on the following scenario:**

C is in charge of a group of 15 people involved in a series of complex projects in the same field. The group has been working together amicably and successfully for a considerable time. Its members value C's leadership.

The next project that the group is expected to carry out has the following activities, time estimates (in months) and precedence's:

| Activity | Precedence | Duration |
|---|---|---|
| A | – | 4 |
| B | – | 3 |
| C | A | 6 |
| D | B | 8 |
| E | C, D | 3 |

**156 In the scenario, the team's stage of development in terms of Tuckman is:**

A Forming

B Storming

C Norming

D Performing

**157 In the scenario, calculate the overall duration of the next project.**

________ **months**

**158 In the scenario, for the next project, the critical path is:**

A A C E

B B D E

C A B D E

D A B C D E

**159 Which THREE of the following are true of a work breakdown structure (WBS)?**

A Breaks complex tasks into manageable pieces

B Sets out the logical sequence of project events

C Specifies the work to be done for each package described

D Is the initial breakdown structure used in planning activities and costs

E Is used to compare different suppliers

F Indicates who is responsible and when the work needs to be delivered

**160 Among project stakeholders, the person/group that is the source of the project manager's authority, and acts as agent of the organisation to ensure that the project achieves its objectives is called:**

A The project owner

B The project customer

C The project champion

D The project sponsor

**161 Which stage of Tuckman's model of team development best applies to the 'identification of a need' phase of the project life cycle?**

A Storming

B Adjourning

C Forming

D Dorming

**162 Which of the following planning techniques takes the form of a component (or 'stacked') vertical bar chart?**

A Gantt chart

B Resource histogram

C Network diagram

D Work breakdown structure

**163 Which tool or technique, which is used for planning the time of a project, is used to measure how far the project has progressed and how far it has to run?**

A Gate

B Milestone

C Critical path

D PERT

**164 Which type of feasibility investigates whether project requirements can be met using available material, technology and processes?**

A Economic

B Social

C Ecological

D Technical

**165 Which THREE of the following are key areas of the Project Management Body of Knowledge (PMBOK)?**

A Integration

B Procurement

C Feasibility

D Human resources

E Planning

F Control

**166 Which of the following statements about the matrix organisation structure is true?**

A It can improve lateral communication and cooperation between specialists

B It can enhance reporting between subordinates and managers

C It can minimise time spent in meetings

D It is most useful where for companies with multiple projects where all the projects are running at the same time

**167 Which of the following is NOT one of the PRINCE2 process areas?**

A Managing stage boundaries

B Managing product delivery

C Risk management

D Controlling

**168 Which of the following project stakeholders is the person who provides the resources for the project?**

A Project sponsor

B Project manager

C Project owner

D Project customer

**169 Identify roles A, B, C and D missing from the basic PRINCE2 project organisational structure from the options below.**

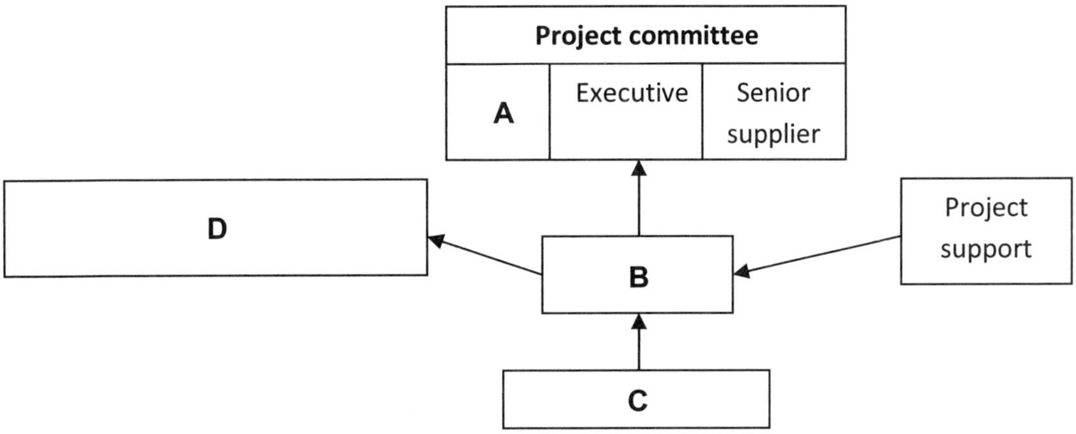


| | | | |
|---|---|---|---|
| Senior user | Project assurance team | Project manager | Stage team leader |

**170** A final report is produced at the end of the project.

Which of the following would NOT be included in the final report?

A Actual achievement in relation to costs and project schedules

B Customer's original requirement and original project deliverable

C The extent to which the benefits defined in the original business case have been achieved

D List of deliverables which the customer received

**171 Which of the following is a benefit of Critical Path Analysis (CPA)?**

A It helps with capacity planning, resource scheduling and management

B Improved quality of systems developed

C Identifies float (or buffer/slack)

D It is drawn in real time

**172 Which of the following factors is a limitation of Gantt charts?**

A Drawn to scale

B Uses real time

C Shows actual durations alongside budget

D They are of limited use when dealing with large project teams

**173** Consider the following network diagram of a simple project.

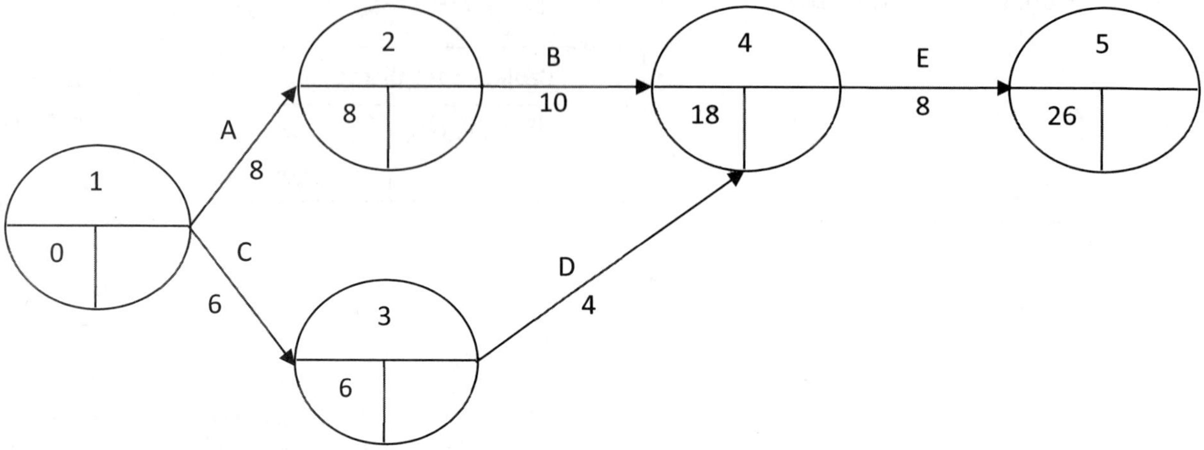


**Calculate the float time on activity C.**

**_____ days**

**174 At what stage in the project life cycle is the scope of a project determined?**

A Planning

B Initiating

C Executing

D Controlling

**175 What is the correct order of Gido and Clements' stages in the project life cycle?**

A Identification of a need, development of a proposed solution, implementation, completion

B Development of a proposed solution, Identification of a need, implementation, completion

C Implementation, completion, identification of a need, development of a proposed solution

D Development of a proposed solution, implementation, completion, identification of a need

**176 Which THREE of the following are key advantages of using project management software?**

A Improved planning and control

B Improved procurement

C Helps with 'what if' analysis

D Access to team members

E Helps in the creation of technical documents

F Reduces project complexity

**177 Which of the following would NOT generally be part of configuration management within a project?**

A Authorisation and tracking of changes

B Version control for documentation

C Access control over project records

D Progress reporting

**178 In a project, when there are conflicting objectives amongst stakeholders, a strategy which implies that both parties must sacrifice something is known as:**

A Negotiation

B Mediation

C Partnering

D Compromise

**179** A key skill required by a project manager is leadership. Blake & Mouton's managerial grid assesses leadership styles along two axes – concern for task performance and concern for people/relationships. Each of these is graded on a scale of 1 to 9.

**Which managerial style did they describe as 'team management'?**

A Very high concern for people and very low concern for the task

B Very high concern for the task and very low concern for people

C Very high concern for people and very high concern for the task

D Very low concern for people and very low concern for the task

**180 Based on the principles of 'one person – one boss' and a decision-making authority, Gido and Clements's project hierarchy is shown below.**

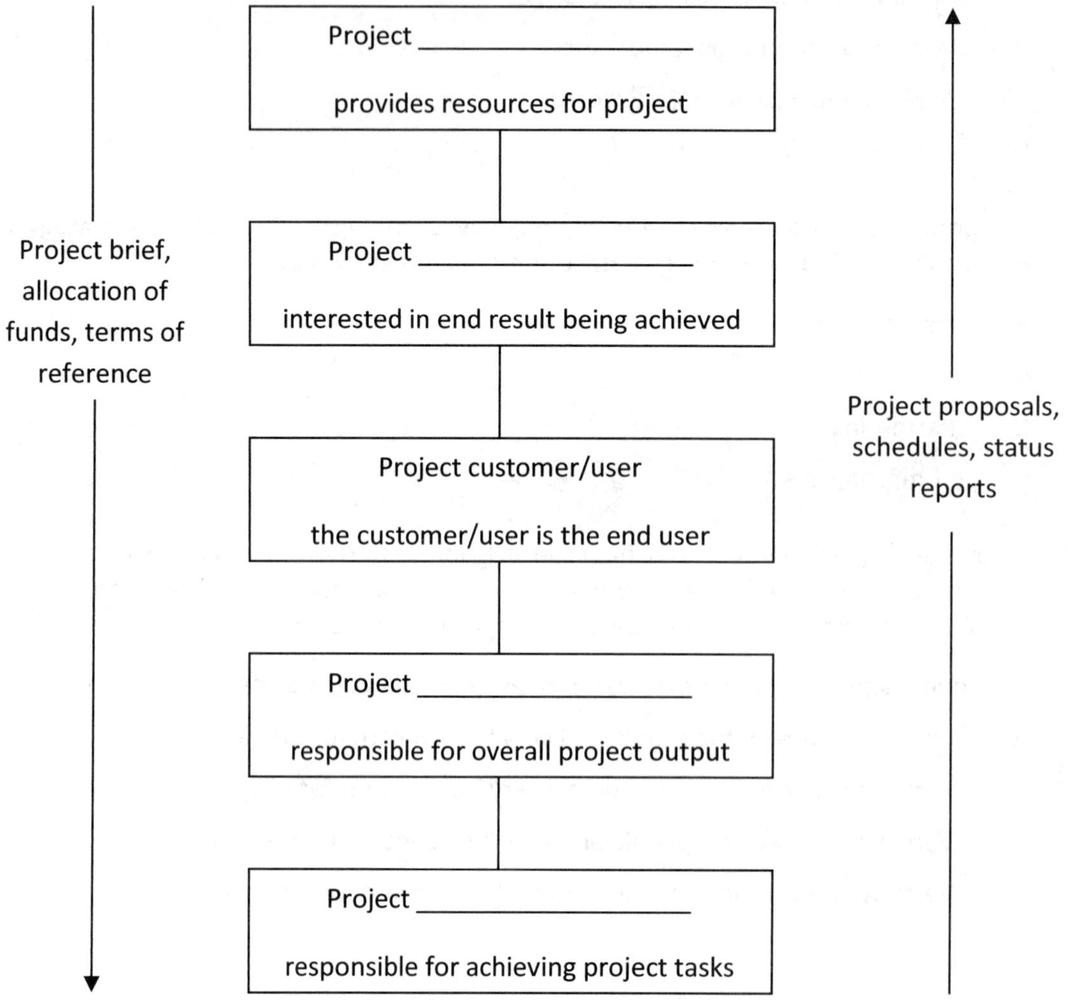


**Complete the diagram by inserting the correct stakeholder from the following options:**

| | | | | | |
|---|---|---|---|---|---|
| owner | manager | sponsor | user | team | champion |

**181 Which of the following activities would NOT be carried out as part of the executing stage of an information systems project?**

A Software testing

B Preparation of training materials

C Installation and changeover procedures

D Carrying out a risk analysis

**182 In the context of the management of disputes within projects, which of the following best describes mediation?**

A To involve the parties discussing the problem

B To create communication links between the project's participants

C To ensure that parties involved in the dispute sacrifice something

D To reach a mutually agreeable solution

**183** Teams are formed to undertake projects. As teams are developing, they go through several stages.

**At which stage of group formation and development does establishing standards and agreeing ways of working occur?**

A Storming

B Performing

C Norming

D Forming

**184 Which of the following statements regarding Gantt charts NOT correct?**

A A Gantt chart can show planned and actual activity durations on the same chart

B A Gantt chart is an alternative or complementary approach to network analysis

C Gantt charts can be used in both planning and control of a project

D A Gantt chart is a stacked, vertical bar chart

**185 Which of the following would be items focused on by a conformance management system?**

A Prioritising change requests, recording of changes and agreement of a change budget

B Functional quality and client satisfaction measures

C Inspection, quality control and quality assurance

D Access control over project records and version control for documentation

**186 Which THREE of the following are used as a control element within projects?**

A Project reports

B Exception reports

C Project meetings

D Feasibility study

E Scenario planning

F PERT

**187 Which of these techniques would be used at the completion stage of a project?**

A Progress reports

B Gantt chart

C External review with customers

D PERT

**188 Which of these meetings would take place regularly with the objective of providing an update on the status of the project?**

A Team meetings

B Progress review meetings

C Problem solving meetings

D Business review meeting

**189 Which of the following is a part of the 'identification of need' stage of the project life cycle?**

A The Completion Report

B The Milestone Review

C Project scheduling

D The Project Initiation Document (PID)

**Questions 190 and 191 are based on the following diagram. Durations are shown in weeks.**

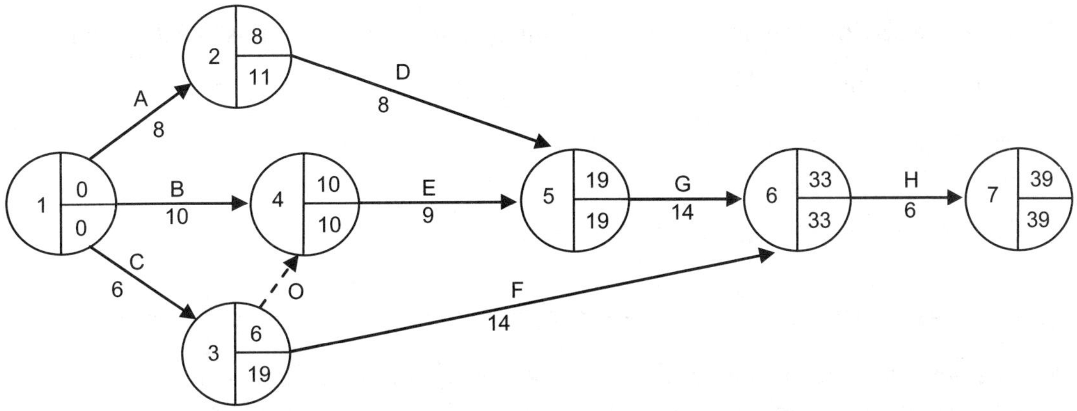


**190 Identify the critical path.**

A ADGH

B CFH

C BEGH

D CEGH

**191 Which THREE of the following statements regarding the diagram are true?**

A The slack on activities C and F is 14 weeks

B If activity E was to overrun, the project duration would increase

C Activity D could take 3 weeks longer and the project would still be completed on time

D Activities A, C and D can start straight away

E If activity H took 10 weeks, the overall duration of the project would be 43 weeks

F Activities A, B and C cannot be carried out at the same time

**192** It is important to identify risks within projects and to consider how these risks can be managed.

**Where a risk is identified as having high likelihood but low impact, the most appropriate risk management approach would be:**

A Transfer

B Avoid

C Reduce

D Accept

**193** When planning for time within a project, account must be taken of risk and uncertainty and there are several techniques which can assist with this.

**Which of the following techniques involves adding artificial slack into risky activities?**

A Scenario planning

B Buffering

C Float

D PERT

**194** Project managers may have to adapt their management style as the project progresses.

**A management approach that focuses on adapting management behaviour to the circumstances of the organisation and to each given situation is known as:**

A Participative leadership

B Scientific management

C Laissez-faire

D Contingency theory

**195** One role of project managers is to motivate the project team.

**If the project manager adopted McGregor's Theory X approach, what would they believe people are motivated by?**

A Money and security

B Achievement at work

C Interpersonal relationships

D Recognition for good work

**196 Which of the following statements about project management software is false?**

A Software can provide a central store for project documentation

B Using software will ensure the project delivers within budget

C The software makes it easier to produce diagrams such as Gantt charts

D The software could include central calendars for managing meetings during the project

**197** One thing is certain in projects and that is change.

**Which of the following are most likely to be affected by change?**

A Project budget

B Project quality

C Project scope

D Project leadership

**198 Which THREE of the following statements regarding the matrix structure are correct?**

A The matrix structure combines the benefits of decentralisation and co-ordination

B Within the matrix structure, employees will have dual reporting lines

C The matrix structure is largely theoretical and is rarely used in practice

D The matrix structure is especially useful when an organisation is undertaking a single large project affecting the whole organisation

E The matrix structure should lead to less duplication across projects and therefore save money

F It works best when projects are relatively simple and inexpensive

**199** Q wishes to initiate new product development in DT Company.

S has assessed a risk to project success. The risk involves an internal shortage of skills to make some of the key components. This risk has been classified as having a low likelihood, but high impact should it arise.

**Identify the most appropriate risk management strategy from the following:**

A Transfer

B Avoid

C Reduce

D Accept

**200** D is a divisional manager in a large construction company. They are responsible for the initiation of divisional projects, approving project plans and making all major project decisions.

**What project stakeholder role does D have?**

A Project owner

B Project sponsor

C Project customer

D Project manager

Section 2

# ANSWERS TO OBJECTIVE TEST QUESTIONS

## BUSINESS MODELS AND VALUE CREATION

**1 C**

The social aspect of PEST(LE) analysis will consider such things as population shifts, age profiles, attitudes, values and beliefs. Cultural or demographic factors would generally be considered under this heading rather than under the political, economic or technological heading. The other two headings are legal and environmental.

**2 The correct matching of the definitions is shown below:**

| | |
|---|---|
| The age at which people are allowed to drink alcohol | Legal |
| Government tax on sales of alcohol | Political |
| The level of disposable income people have | Economic |
| People's religious beliefs and attitudes towards alcohol | Social |

**3 C**

The relatively low cost of the machine and licence, together with the fact that an unskilled person would only require a two-day training course suggests that it would fairly easy for anyone to enter the market. Using the five forces model would conclude that the threat of new entrants is high.

No information is given in the question regarding the powers of the buyers or suppliers or the rivalry within the industry.

**4** The force which would consider this information is **Rivalry amongst competitors** and from the scenario, the force would be **High**.

The threat from rivals will be high as the four main players are similar size and account for the majority of the market. The leading company holds 26% of the market. In addition, the market is growing slowly therefore to make inroads into this market it will require to take some market share from one of the main players which they would resist strongly.

**5 C**

Numerous suppliers would suggest that supplier power is low and in terms of barriers to entry, if anything this would enhance the likelihood of entering the market.

**6 A, B and D**

Barriers to entry to a market are those aspects which make it difficult for a new company to enter the market. Potential entrants to the market will want the barriers to be low, but existing companies operating in the market will want the barriers to be high to stop new entrants coming into the market and intensifying competition.

**7 B**

Competitors will need to sell a lot to cover high fixed costs so will fight aggressively to maximise sales and cover their fixed costs.

Rapid growth in the market would make existing competition less intense, as existing competitors would struggle to keep up with demand and would not need to acquire competitor's customers to grow.

Relative quality and costs of similar products drives the threat of substitute products.

High barriers to entry would affect the threat of new entrants.

**8 D**

It will be difficult for new companies to enter this market. This is mainly due to the accreditation that is required before a company can offer courses, and this process can take several years.

**9 B**

The existence of patents makes it harder for new companies to enter the market.

The others would all make it easier or more attractive to enter the market.

**10 C**

Threat of substitutes refers to people's tendency to replace one product with another.

**11 A**

According to Porter, organisations can generate competitive advantage through:

- Cost leadership – offering the same quality as competitors but at a lower price.
- Differentiation – offering innovative and high-quality products which can be differentiated from rival products and for which high prices can be gained.
- Focus – concentrating on a small, niche part of the market.

**12 B**

Big data refers to the large volume of data (Volume), many sources and types of data (Variety), and the speed at which data is being generated and the rate at which it needs to be processed and analysed (Velocity). Option A is incorrect in that big data does not refer to any specific financial amount. Option C is also incorrect. Big data does come from many sources, but this is too narrow a definition. Option D is incorrect as big data contains both financial and non-financial data.

**13 D**

By definition

**14 C**

This is a description of artificial intelligence and machine learning.

**15 A, B and D**

To increase security and address the issue of cyber risk, all the transactions in a blockchain are publicly available and all transactions must be verified by a decentralised network of computers (not by individuals). Cryptocurrencies are one of the many applications that run on the blockchain, but they are not an example of blockchain.

**16 B, C and F**

The IBM report 'The New Age of Ecosystems' suggested that emerging technologies create an environment that is connected and open, simple and intelligent, fast and scalable.

**17 B**

'Reach' refers to a participant's ability to extend activity or interactions throughout the environment.

**18 D**

'Course' refers to the speed and direction at which content or value is exchanged within an ecosystem. Jessie's business model relies on a high-speed transfer of information and value.

**19 B**

Statement (i) is false – in traditional markets we assume that entities act out of individual self-interest but within ecosystems value creation is seen to be more collaborative.

Statement (ii) is true as ecosystems only exist because participants can deliver more value acting together for the mutual benefit. This results in higher levels of coordination, shared ideals, shared standards and shared goals, than in traditional markets.

**20 B**

The specialist nature of Wimber's skills is indicative of high barriers to entry within the industry and, hence high complexity. The presence of extensive regulation would suggest rules-based transactions and tight orchestration.

**21 D**

Barriers to entry, and hence complexity, are low, yet orchestration (by the regulator) is high, indicating a wolf pack ecosystem.

**22 A**

Brand atomization is when organisations need to design their offerings so that they can be more widely distributed and be part of the platform that is offered by other providers.

**23 C**

According to the World Economic Forum/Accenture analysis, there is greater instance these days of customers attaching more importance to independent reviews of products or services than to marketing information provided by the business or reviews from other organisations (such as trade journals). The purchase decision will be influenced by what fellow customers have said, meaning that a poor review can have a disastrous effect on future sales potential. This is known as 'peer review and advocacy'.

**24 A**

Defining value is when organisations look at who they create value for and what counts as value for them.

**25 B**

Stakeholders with low interest and high power can easily increase their level of interest which would make them key to any decisions being made. The best way to manage such stakeholders is to keep them satisfied in order to keep them from moving from quadrant III to quadrant IV.

**26** The employees would have high interest and low power therefore the correct strategy for managing them would be **keep informed**.

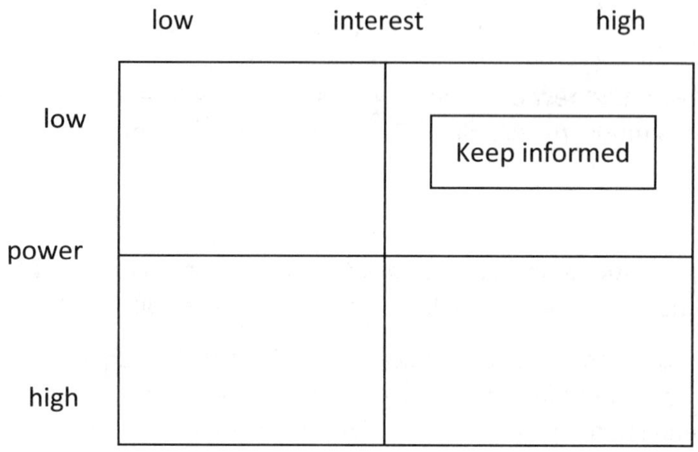


**27 A**

The objective is to prevent this group from joining forces with other, more powerful groups. It is important with this group that the activities of the organisation are presented as rational so that the group gain an understanding as to the reasons behind the organisation's actions.

Minimal effort would be used for stakeholders with low power and low interest.

Keep satisfied would be used for stakeholders with high power and low interest.

Key player would be used for stakeholders with high power and high interest.

**28 D**

Key suppliers score highly on all three attributes:

Legitimacy – the suppliers are entitled to go to court and seek a winding up order in the circumstances described

Urgency – key suppliers have already served notice of their intent

Power – the court may initiate a winding up order if the company doesn't act accordingly

**29 B**

Statement (i) is false – the cost model includes actual as well as expected costs.

Statement (ii) is true – sharing value is based on the principle of creating shared value, which comprises shareholder value and the value delivered to other stakeholders. The pecking order depends on the seasons and cycles of firms and their operating environment. At least four stakeholder groups are in view: government (taxes); shareholders (dividends); incentives for executives (performance-related pay); and the firm (retained income for reinvestments). The sharing has to be sensitive to the interactions in the operating environment so that it does not harm the firm's reputation, or the creation and delivery of further value. The key bases for decision-making here are thus: tax strategy, dividend policy, desired capital structure and investment opportunities.

**30 B**

Desirable segments typically have customers who make few or no returns.

**31 A, C and E**

Customer segments can be based on geography (where they live); demography (gender, age, marital status, income), lifestyle (cultural practices, social values), behaviour (previous purchase history, product benefits sought, preferred means of interaction) and purchase journey (how they made purchase decisions, who was responsible for their spend, how they talked about the brand and purchase).

B is thus a geographic basis for segmentation, D a lifestyle one and F a behaviour one.

**32 D**

Although the customer buying journey can be fluid, complex and involve multiple channels, those channels must be integrated into a seamless experience.

**33 A**

The cost architecture is established when defining value and involves four key factors:

- Efficiency of the processes.
- Levels of activity.
- Resources consumed during activities.
- Price paid for resources.

Investment opportunities (B) and dividend policy (C) are a consideration when sharing residual value and collection policy (D) is part of the revenue model.

**34 C**

Value is not just another word for profit (A) and includes financial and non-financial aspects. Intangible value (B) is growing in importance, so companies should focus on it as well as tangible aspects. Creating value is not just about increasing shareholder wealth (D) – the whole point of ecosystems is the idea of creating shared value that goes beyond shareholders.

**35 B**

Statement (i) is false – **formulating** a value proposition that meet the needs of the high priority stakeholders is a key aspect of **defining** value rather than creating it.

Statement (ii) is true.

**36**

| **Element** | **YourFuture** |
|---|---|
| Partners | YourFuture's ecosystem includes university departments, local authorities, map providers and businesses. |
| Resources | YourFuture uses its relationships with various employers to source the information needed for the web portal. |
| Processes | YourFuture has designed a system where potential employers can populate information directly into the web portal. |
| Activities | YourFuture uses a workflow system to allocate tasks and for operational reporting. |
| Outputs | The e-learning platform for teachers, as they are key customers. |

**37**

| Category | Strategy |
|---|---|
| Cryptocurrency | Buyers of gaming supplies (headsets, controllers, chairs etc.) from a range of retail websites can pay for those supplies using 'Creds', earned by winning online multi-player games. |
| Platform | Car manufacturers that are members of DriveIT are sharing data collected from car operating systems with one-another, to improve the ways that all their vehicles operate and promote the sale of car-related products and services. |
| Fintech | PlaceIT is a portfolio management platform – taking business away from typically person-to-person advisers. Subscribers can use a smartphone app to get advice and manage their investment portfolio. |
| IoT (Internet of Things) | SwitchITon provides customers with a device and app that interconnect all of their domestic appliances and allow them to be controlled remotely. |

A cryptocurrency is a digital form of money, meeting the attributes of a store of value, unit of account and medium of exchange.

A platform is a de-centralised and interactive collection of related services, often available globally, that uses Internet technologies such as cloud and mobile.

Finance Technologies (Fintech) are completely disrupting the traditional banking sector – long seen as a highly technical, highly regulated industry dominated by giant banks.

The IoT is the connected network of consumer and industrial non-IT hardware. It includes, but is not limited to, vehicles, factory machinery, domestic appliances and buildings.

**38 C**

The Internet of Me – users are being placed at the centre of digital experiences through apps and services being personalised.

**39 D**

The Platform (r)evolution – global platforms are becoming easier to establish and cheaper to run. Developments such as cloud computing and mobile technology offer huge potential for innovation and quicker delivery of next-generation services. The rate of evolution is only going to increase.

**40 D**

In order for an organisation to properly take advantage of a move to digital, or to survive digital disruption within its industry, the executive leadership team will need to demonstrate a number of abilities:

**Inspirational leadership** – digitisation will be an exercise in change management, but probably on a bigger and quicker scale than the organisation will typically be used to. The leadership team will need to energise the workforce and inspire confidence that digitisation is the right way forwards and is being carried out in the right way.

**Competitive edge** – not only will the leadership need to motivate others within the organisation to see the digital transformation as the right strategy; they will also have to persuade people to potentially change their mindset.

**Establishing a strategic direction** – this is probably something that the business has done for a long time, but a digital strategy may require it to be done in a different way. For example, the planning horizon may need to be shortened, or greater flexibility introduced – perhaps a move away from the rational model to a more emergent approach, which would enable the business to adapt as time passes.

**Influence external parties** – for example, providers of finance. Raising capital is likely to be necessary, but showing how that capital may be applied and the value that will result might be more problematic. Will investing in cloud technology deliver increased shareholder wealth? If so, how much? And when? There will be greater uncertainty over outcomes, and the leaders of the business will need to be persuasive and articulate a compelling value proposition.

**Collaboration** – the organisation will need to see itself as part of a wider ecosystem if it is to deliver the requisite value. This will require careful thought on who to collaborate with and how each part of the ecosystem will contribute.

**Business judgement** – what sort of business model will the organisation need to put in place? It is probable that an altogether different model to what has worked in the past will be required.

**Execution** – having determined what technologies can help to drive the business forwards, thought must then be given to how these can be used most effectively by the people within the business. People and technology need to work in harmony to produce the desired outcomes.

**Building talent** – it will be critical to identify the skills that staff will need to demonstrate and to manage training/recruitment to ensure that the business has those skills. New roles are likely to be required, including at the most senior level – for example, perhaps a new board position of Chief Digital Officer.

**Note**: 'Influence external parties' and 'collaboration' are externally focused. The other six abilities are more internally focused.

**41 A**

Establishing a strategic direction – this is probably something that the business has done for a long time, but a digital strategy may require it to be done in a different way. For example, the planning horizon may need to be shortened, or greater flexibility introduced – perhaps a move away from the rational model to a more emergent approach, which would enable the business to adapt as time passes.

**42 C**

Cate is demonstrating an ability to **influence external parties** – notably, providers of finance. Raising capital is likely to be necessary, but showing how that capital may be applied and the value that will result might be more problematic. Will investing in cloud technology deliver increased shareholder wealth? If so, how much? And when? There will be greater uncertainty over outcomes, and the leaders of the business will need to be persuasive and articulate a compelling value proposition.

**43 B**

**Building** new business models might be the best route when an opportunity is related to the company's core business. The benefits are that it typically maximises control and minimises costs in markets that a company must own because of their strategic importance. If companies decide to go for the build route, they can benefit by creating and developing new products and services.

**44 A**

A firm can use **partnering** with a digital disruptor to learn more about the market and its partner's model. A partnering approach is sensible when it makes sense to learn about emergent opportunities, with an eye toward deeper partnerships or acquisitions in the future. Companies need to develop a more flexible and open mind-set toward partnerships; which are expected to play an important role in the digital transformation of market players.

**45 D**

**Invest** in interesting start-ups is often a valid option, allowing an established company to connect with the right skills and capabilities. It will also avoid hindering entrepreneurial forces with a setup focused on internal governance and reporting.

**46 B**

Investment and incubation/acceleration might seem similar endeavours. The latter however represents a closer relationship to the funding company, deploying corporate internal capabilities, infrastructure and resources to the start-ups. Having said that, incubators and accelerators need to precisely outline both internal benefits and incentives for start-ups and entrepreneurs, and a clear strategy and vision.

**47 B, D and E**

The five DTI business models are customer-centric, extra-frugal, data-powered, Skynet and open and liquid.

Cost leadership (A) is one of Porter's generic strategies. Market development (C) is one of Ansoff's strategies for growth. Build (F) is a possible business model.

**48 A**

**Data-powered.** This model is built around prowess in analytics and software intelligence. Epitomized by Google and Netflix, data-powered companies have an agile culture focused on innovation through empirical experimentation.

**49 C**

Skynet. Named after the conscious, artificial general intelligence of the Terminator films, this model makes intensive use of machines to increase productivity and flexibility in production. Pioneered by enterprises such as Amazon and Rio Tinto, Skynet organizations are characterized by an engineer-led culture dedicated to automation.

**50 By definition:**

| Operating model | Description |
|---|---|
| Customer-centric | This model focuses on making customers' lives easier and emphasises front-office processes. It works best with a culture that puts the client first and a decentralised structure that empowers frontline staff. |
| Extra-frugal | This model thrives on a culture of 'less is more' and a standardised organisational structure. By optimising manufacturing, supply and support processes, it can provide a high-quality service at a low cost. |
| Data-powered | This model is built around prowess in analytics and software intelligence. Data-powered companies have an agile culture focused on innovation through empirical experimentation. |
| Skynet | This model makes intensive use of machines to increase productivity and flexibility in production. Skynet organisations are characterised by an engineer-led culture dedicated to automation. |
| Open and liquid | This model looks outward with a view to creating an ecosystem that can enrich the customer proposition. Built around a sharing customer, all processes are characterised by a constant flow of dialogue with the outside world. |

**51 C**

Attracting and retaining talent starts by listening to what employees are saying about a firm, both externally and internally. Referred employees perform better, so enterprises should incentivize their employees to use online networks to refer potential employees.

**52 B**

KTJ is creating a workforce with digital skills. Organisations need to actively develop the skills they need in-house by making training a critical component of their talent management strategy. Bring new skills into the organization by hiring digital leaders and digital natives.

**53 D**

L Company is trying to foster a digital culture in the enterprise. Factors that set a digital company's culture apart include a strong sense of purpose and a diverse high-quotient digital workforce. Leadership needs to release people's creativity and apply lean start-up methodologies such as hackathons and design thinking.

**54 A**

Statement (i) is true.

Statement (ii) is false – firms need to make greater use of long-term goals rather than short term ones.

**55**

| **Force** | **Effect** |
|---|---|
| Bargaining power of suppliers | Remain stable |
| Bargaining power of customers | Remain stable |
| Rivalry | Decrease |
| Threat of new entrants | Decrease |

As Charlton already has mutually beneficial relationships with customers and suppliers, the adoption of an ecosystem approach is unlikely to have any significant effect on those forces. The most likely impact, if successful, would be to gain Charlton advantage over rivals, as none of them currently take this approach, thus decreasing rivalry. Due to the cost and time involved in establishing an ecosystem approach, a barrier to entry would be created, thus decreasing the threat of new entrants.

**56 B**

A business ecosystem can be defined as 'an economic community supported by a foundation of interacting organisations and individuals — the organisms of the business world.'

**57 B, D and E**

Regulatory frameworks are being challenged by ecosystems on several fronts – these include:

- **Speed of change** (B) – effective regulation depends upon the regulators' understanding of the solutions being offered by businesses, their efficacy, and their possible unintended consequences.
- **Innovators find a back door** (not an answer choice)
- **Ecosystems evolve** (D) and new and clever business models proliferate, the sheer diversity of competitors and competitive modes is yet another complicating factor for regulators.
- **Innovations cross lines of jurisdiction** (E) and in business ecosystems, product definitions, market boundaries, the traditional distinction between digital and physical goods blur.

The high cost of new legislation (A), the need for data protection (C), and customers demanding a more personalised experience (F) are all general challenges that are not specific to regulating ecosystems.

## 58 A, C and D

Traditional industries such as high street banking and the newspaper industry have now been replaced by online versions and apps. Music is also now being downloaded or streamed instantly.

Social media interactions (B) have increased, the costs have declined for manufacturers as the technologies develop (E), and connectivity with customers is faster (F).

## 59 D

Use of mobile technology has reduced duplication and data entry. App software for logging and recording expenses has reduced manual processing, whilst delivering significant efficiencies and better-quality management information.

## 60 D

Digital assets are assets held by a business in digital form that do not have physical substance.

# MANAGING PEOPLE PERFORMANCE

## 61 A, B and F

For an individual it provides feedback about performance and assessment of competence (A), provides a basis for remuneration (B) an identifies training and development needs (F).

C and D are advantages for an organisation, whereas E is an advantage of a robust reward system.

## 62 B

The 360 approach gives individuals the opportunity to appraise their manager and (perhaps) their colleagues. Knowing that this will take place encourages individuals to work together for the good of the department (B).

The Ranking System focuses on pre-agreed targets (A), the Unstructured Format approach aims to capture all aspects of performance (C) and the subordinate would appraise his own performance (D) in the "Self-Rating approach.

## 63 C

As the employees rarely go onto the intranet, X has picked the wrong communication channel.

There is no evidence that the message was poorly encoded/structured or that the other members of staff could not understand the message (decode it).

There is also no evidence that anything has been interfering with the communication or making it difficult to understand, so noise is not an obvious problem.

**64 The most appropriate action for each of the employees is shown below:**

| | |
|---|---|
| Employee 1 | Suspension without pay |
| Employee 2 | An informal talk |
| Employee 3 | An oral warning |
| Employee 4 | Dismissal, demotion or transfer |

**65 The correct matching is:**

There is one best way to undertake every task – **Taylor's scientific management**

Interpersonal relations are a key part of determining workplace behaviour – **Human relations school**

Managers must control the needs of the task, individual and group – **Adair's action-centred leadership**

Managers can be either a psychologically distant or psychologically close – **Fiedler's contingency theory**

**66 A, B and E**

Drucker suggested eight key objectives which a business would need to cover all areas where performance and results affect the business. These are: profitability, innovation, market standing, productivity, financial and physical resources, managerial performance and development, worker performance and attitude and public responsibility.

**67 C**

An effective staff appraisal system can bring many benefits, both to the organisation and to the individual. While it can improve communication, identify training needs and provide a fair process for reward decision, it cannot ensure that performance targets are met.

**68 D**

Centralisation involves most decisions being made centrally within the organisation (i.e. at head office level).

This means less training for more junior/local staff as well as better goal congruence as all decisions within the organisation are made by the same, senior group of managers.

Options (ii) and (iii) are advantages of decentralisation.

**69 B**

The employee is responsible for his or her own health and safety. The employer has a duty to provide a safe working environment.

**70 B**

Intrinsic satisfaction is derived from the job content. Extrinsic satisfaction is derived from factors separate to the job itself and is dependent on the decisions of others. Pay, working conditions and benefits are all examples of extrinsic rewards.

**71 D**

In fact, the manager is using legitimate power, because they are only able to promote someone by virtue of their formal authority to do so. Of the options given, however, reward power is the only one that applies: it resides in the manager's ability to influence the subordinate's behaviour by controlling potential promotions (whether the subordinate is promoted). Referent power is the power to inspire followership in others; to lead by personal charisma.

**72 The complete model is shown below:**

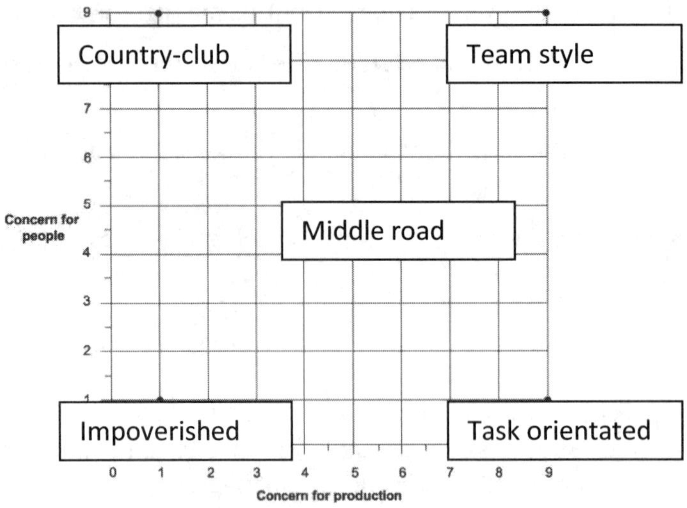


**73 The correct matching is:**

These help to avoid unpleasantness and dissatisfaction – **Hygiene factor**

Good working conditions – **Hygiene factor**

An appropriate level of salary – **Hygiene factor**

Career advancement – **Motivator**

These satisfy the need for personal growth – **Motivator**

**74 C**

Disciplinary action is usually 'progressive': that is, warnings – and subsequent sanctions – become increasingly severe with each failure to adjust performance.

**75 A**

A grievance procedure occurs when an employee feels that their superior or colleagues are wrongly treating them. Having a good grievance procedure in place will help ensure the legal obligations of the employer are met (A) and improves (not reduces as in B) employee morale and trust. However, it will not ensure all employees will follow instructions (C) and it does not reduce the number of customer complaints about staff (D).

**76** The correct matching is:

| Task | Individual | Group |
|---|---|---|
| • Opinion-seeking | • Employee feedback | • Peace keeping |
| • Decision making | • Employee counselling | • Communicating |

**77 B, E and F**

Goals, skills and technology would be visible elements, but attitudes, style and values would be hidden elements.

**78 C**

McGregor's Theory X and Theory Y are attitudes based on social science research, and McGregor regarded them as two distinct attitudes. Theory X is based on assumptions such as the dislike of individuals for work, which means that they must be controlled and threatened by their supervisors and managers. McGregor believed that Theory Y was difficult to apply in some working conditions, such as mass production operations, and that it was much better suited to the management of managers and other professionals.

**79 A**

Personal centralised control (A) is often found in small, owner-managed organisations. In these organisations, control is carried out by the owner through personal supervision.

Output control (B) is based on the measurement of outputs and is often used in manufacturing organisations.

Clan or cultural control (C) is found in organisations where the employees have a strong identification with management goals, and they are given a degree of freedom in how they carry out their tasks.

Bureaucratic control (D) is based on formal rules and procedures and is often found in large hierarchical organisations.

**80 C**

Managing health and safety is not solely the responsibility of directors (C). While senior management have a legal requirement to comply with the Health and Safety legislation, all employees also have responsibility towards health and safety.

Managing health and safety in the workplace is a legal requirement in the UK (A) and the requirements are covered by the Health and Safety at work act 1974 (HASAWA).

Cost savings can be made from compliance with health and safety legislation (B). This comes from lower legal costs for compensation and lower costs due to fewer workdays lost by employees.

One of the key areas of the HASAWA is provision of information, training and instruction of staff in areas of health and safety (D).

**81 The correct matching is:**

- Its purpose is to remove discrimination – Equal opportunities
- It relies on proactive action – Equal opportunities
- It is a Human Resources role – Equal opportunities
- It is a managerial role – Diversity

**82 C**

Contingency theory sees effective leadership as being dependent on a number of variable or contingent factors – in Adair's case these variables are task needs, individual needs and group needs.

Adair's model looks at leadership in relation to the needs of the task, individual and group.

**83 B**

This would be the definition of the role of a mentor.

**84 A, D and F**

Traditional authority is based on Weber's classical bureaucracy. This is incorrect. Traditional authority is based on custom and practice. Rational-legal authority is based on Weber's classical bureaucracy.

Responsibility is the capacity to exert influence. This is incorrect. This is the definition of power.

Accountability (not authority) requires individuals to justify any failure to fulfil their responsibilities to their superiors.

**85 The complete sentence is:**

Under UK law, the director could bring an action for **wrongful** or **unfair** dismissal.

An action for wrongful dismissal is an action for breach of contract of employment: here the contract provides for one year's notice of termination. The director can, alternatively, bring a statutory claim for unfair dismissal under the Employment Rights Act.

**86 D**

The focus of Taylor's model is that staff members should be scientifically chosen to ensure they are suitable for the job they are being hired to do.

Once hired, management are responsible for all key decisions and providing instructions to workers. While co-operation between workers and managers should be close, scientific management does not suggest employee suggestion schemes.

**87 D**

J's position is clearly unfavourable, with little power and a poor relationship with her staff. Psychologically distant leaders favour formal roles and relationships, judge subordinates based on performance and are primarily task oriented. This would best for J.

In contrast psychologically close leaders do not seek to formalise roles and relationships and are more concerned with maintaining good relationships at work. Their style works best when the situation is moderately favourable.

**88 A**

The human relations approach suggests that relationship and interactions are more important to creating a productive workforce than money or imposed standards.

**89 C**

The work of human resources staff is usually hard to quantify, however they have a significant influence on the income a company generates and therefore it is presumed that they should share a part of the profit.

**90 A, B and C**

Staff bonuses mean that the manager is offering her staff a reward for adopting the system. As a manger, she has legitimate power. She is also relying on referent power by using her charisma/relationship with her employees. She is not planning to use coercive or expert power. Autocratic is not one of the types of power.

**91 C**

The Equality Act 2010 covers the following grounds for discrimination:

- Age
- Disability
- Gender reassignment
- Marriage and civil partnership
- Pregnancy and maternity
- Race
- Religion or belief
- Sex
- Sexual orientation

It does not cover discrimination due to physical appearance.

**92 C**

There is a subtle point here. The delegator must 'back off' in the sense of not constantly checking on or interfering with the subordinate in his or her use of the delegated authority: this would not be genuine delegation at all. However, the point is not to leave the subordinate without guidance or assistance where it may be required: it is important that the delegator be available. The other options are features of effective delegation: note that it is a thoroughly collaborative process.

**93 D, E and F**

There are limited grounds for redundancy. Redundancy can occur where a role is no longer required. Roles become redundant and this is not linked to individual conduct or performance. Where there is cessation of a business or part of a business or of certain activities within a business then redundancy can be justified.

**94 C**

Accountability is about 'answering to' or 'reporting to' more senior. It is an upward requirement. Authority is the 'right' of someone (often by virtue of their position in the hierarchy) to make decisions or give orders. Empowerment is the process whereby greater authority and discretion (and corresponding responsibility) is given to lower levels in the organisation. Super-ordination is a process whereby something is 'higher' than something else in a hierarchy or arrangement: we talk about 'super-ordinate goals', for example, for those at a higher level in the hierarchy of plans.

**95 A**

There are three levels of control: Strategic, Tactical and Operational.

At the strategic level, the board will set the control environment. Policies for control, such as recruitment, selection, appraisal and discipline will be set.

At the tactical level, the decisions of the board will be implemented. Procedures for controlling recruitment, selection, appraisal and discipline will be established and monitored.

At the operational level, operational controls will be designed to control structured repetitive activities. This could cover activities such as inventory control or ordering systems.

**96 C, E and F**

'Values' are the things which can be identified from stories and the opinions of those within the organisation. It includes items such as language used, behaviour and how people justify what they do.

The things that can be seen, heard and observed are 'Artefacts'. Deeply held beliefs are known as 'Basic assumptions' and 'the way we do things around here' is Handy's overall definition of culture.

**97 C**

Strong cultures can become very set in their ways and as such can affect the organisation's ability to change considering changes in the environment.

Answers A, B and D are usually seen as advantages of strong cultures.

**98 B**

Morgan argued that we need to be able view organisations from a range of different perspectives in order to understand and improve effectiveness and that three key perspectives were organisations as machines, organisations as organisms and organisations as cultures.

**99 B, D and E**

It is important to remember that responsibility cannot be delegated, but authority must be delegated along with the task in question. Option C is incorrect as the scope of responsibility must correspond to the scope of the authority given. Option F is incorrect as this is the definition of empowerment.

**100 A, D and F**

In principle, the more training days (A) an employee receives the more knowledgeable and skilful he or she becomes.

A target for the percentage of total sales revenue earned from new products or services (D) focuses on innovation. The higher the target percentage, the more innovative the organisation might be with new product development.

The number of new product design ideas per employee (F) would be an appropriate measure of innovation.

**101 B**

The indicators in the prompt that confirm G as a completer-finisher include the phrases 'keen eye for detail', identifies minor details in documents that others miss', 'always meets his deadlines' and 'reluctant to involve others'. These are consistent with Belbin's descriptions of the contributions that the completer-finisher can make, as well as possible weaknesses.

Like the completer-finisher, the implementer is disciplined and reliable but is typified by being prepared to take concepts and ideas and then put them into practical effect. The monitor-evaluator considers all alternatives and often displays good judgement but may lack personal drive. The shaper is good under pressure and challenges the team to achieve its goals.

**102 The correct matching is shown below:**

| | |
|---|---|
| Horizontal | Occurs between departments at the same level in the organisation |
| Vertical | Occurs between individuals and groups at different levels |
| Constructive | Considered positive and beneficial to the organisation |
| Destructive | Tends to cause alienation between groups and individuals |

**103 B**

Norming establishes the norms under which the group will operate. This includes how the group will take decisions, behaviour patterns, levels of trust and openness and individual roles.

**104 D**

Contingency theorists do not ignore the lessons learnt from earlier theorists – they adapt them.

**105 A – Plant**

**B – Monitor-evaluator**

**C – Team worker**

The plant role is played by a creative individual; the monitor-evaluator is good at making accurate judgements, whereas the team worker looks after the atmosphere within the team.

**106 A**

This characteristic helps to win positions or gain victories at the other's expense rather than meet the needs of both parties. It is more likely to result in a lose-lose strategy.

**107 C, E and F**

The finance department can help ensure a profitable selling price is used for EFG's products. Finance will also help set the budget for the sales volume in order to produce the sales budget. They will also provide marketing with information to help determine EFG's market share for various products.

**108 A**

Teams tend to be slower at making decisions than individuals, as there are more people involved in the decision-making process. This also means that decisions are often compromises when made in teams. However, the involvement of more people in the decision-making process means that teams have better control – there are a number of people to review the decisions being made.

**109 The correct matching is:**

This technique involves the conflicting party directly engaging with each other and negotiating with one another to try to work out their differences – **Confrontation**.

This technique involves management imposing shared targets on both parties which will require the cooperation of both parties in order to meet the target – **Superordinate goals**.

With this technique, members of one department will be asked to work in the other department for a period, to allow them to better understand the issues faced by the other department – **Member rotation**.

A technique which can be used where conflicting parties are uncooperative is to bring in an independent party to meet with the conflicting parties to encourage them to reach agreement – **Third party consultants**.

**110 D**

Groupthink involves an unwavering belief in the group and its decisions and a sectarian emphasis on agreement.

The Abilene paradox is a famous case which demonstrates that a group can end up with an outcome that none of the individual members wanted.

Risky shift refers to the tendency for groups to make decisions which are riskier than any of the individual members would take on their own.

Conformity refers to the situation where group members are persuaded by the group to agree with decisions which are obviously wrong, and which they know to be wrong.

**111 C**

The correct order for the negotiation process is preparation, opening, bargaining, and closing.

**112 The correct matching is shown below:**

**A Suppression**

**B Resolution**

**C Reduction**

**D Stimulation and orchestration**

Conflict stimulation and orchestration. This approach actively encourages conflict as a means of generating new ideas and new approaches or of stimulating change.

Conflict suppression. This involves the use or threatened use of authority or force, the avoidance of recognition that a conflict situation exists, or smoothing over the conflict by de-emphasising the seriousness of the situation.

Conflict reduction. This involves building on areas of agreement and on common objectives, and changing attitudes and perceptions of the parties involved.

Conflict resolution. This seeks to eliminate the root causes of conflict by establishing a consensus.

**113 The correct matching is shown below:**

**A Reciprocity**

**B Scarcity**

**C Social proof**

**D Liking**

Reciprocity – Remind the person of things you have done for them in the past.

Social proof – Use the opinions of those already supporting you to influence other to join that support.

Scarcity – Advise people that they could lose out if they don't act quickly.

Liking – Building relationships with the people you want to influence so that they trust you.

**114 A**

Statement 2 is the definition of 'style' theories.

**115 B**

In Belbin's model, it is not necessary for different individuals to carry each role; one person can undertake more than one role. It is just necessary that all the roles are covered.

**116 D**

In the forming stage, the team comes together. In the next stage (storming), the group reassesses its targets and roles via more or less open conflict. Norming is a period of settling down, where the group establishes norms and ways of working. In the performing stage, the team transfers its energies to task performance. If the team remains for a long time at the performing stage, there is a danger that it can become less effective as it starts to operate on 'automatic pilot'. If this happens it is best to adjourn the group.

**117 The completed sentences are:**

**Reference groups** are those the individual does not currently belong to but wants to join.

**Informal groups** are those in which membership is normally voluntary and informal.

**Formal groups (or teams) are created by the organisation to carry out specific tasks, communicate and solve problems.**

**Self-directed groups** are encouraged to manage their own work and practices.

**118 C**

A win: win approach which seeks to benefit all parties is known as collaborating. This approach is used when there is high assertiveness and high cooperativeness. The goal with compromising is to find a middle ground, however this can be seen as a 'lose-lose' since neither party gets what it really wants. Competing is a 'win-lose' approach and accommodating is a 'lose-win' approach.

**119 B**

The way words are said can be more important than the actual words themselves.

**120 D**

This is the definition of negotiation.

**121 The correct matching is shown below:**

| | |
|---|---|
| Plant | Imaginative and very good at coming up with original ideas and suggestions. |
| Completer Finisher | Gives attention to detail and is concerned with meeting deadlines. |
| Team Worker | Supports other members of the team and helps to promote harmony. |

**122 A**

Mainwaring suggested four conflict managing strategies: suppression, resolution, reduction and stimulation and orchestration.

**123 D**

Norming means agreeing who should be doing what and establishing modes of behaviour, with team relationships becoming settled. The project manager will begin to pass control and authority for decision-making to the team members.

**124 C**

Large pay rises are a classic 'ego' factor. Pension schemes and permanent contracts will give the employee security, while covering living (or essential) costs is a basic need.

**125 A**

The shaper is described as someone who is committed to the task, may be aggressive and challenging, will always promote activity. The plant is the thoughtful and thought-provoking individual, the team worker is concerned with the relationships within the group, and the completer finisher is the progress chaser who ensures deadlines are met.

**126 The correct order is shown below:**

| | |
|---|---|
| 1 | Preparation |
| 2 | Opening |
| 3 | Bargaining |
| 4 | Closing |

**127 A, B and E**

Vaill suggested the following five characteristics were shared by high performance teams.

- Clarification of broad purposes and short-term objectives.
- Commitment to purposes.
- Teamwork focused on the task at hand.
- Strong and clear leadership.
- Generation of inventions and new methods.

**128 D**

With distributed leadership, leadership is shared so that team members effectively interact and lead each other. It is more horizontal in nature, compared to traditional leadership which is more vertical or hierarchical. Autocratic and free rein are both leadership styles and would not be horizontal in nature.

**129 The correct matching is shown below:**

| | |
|---|---|
| Conformity | Individuals within the group can be persuaded to accept decisions which they know to be wrong |
| Abilene paradox | The group can end up with an outcome which none of the members wanted |
| Risky shift | Groups can end up taking decisions which are riskier than the individual members would take |
| Groupthink | Group members reach consensus without critically testing, analysing and evaluating ideas |

**130 C**

Synergy is often described as 2 + 2 = 5.

**131 The complete sentences are:**

Where boundaries between departments are not clearly defined, this can cause problems of **interdependencies**.

Communication problems can lead to **misunderstandings**.

**History** suggests that conflict tends to be self-perpetuating.

**132 The correct matching is shown below:**

| | |
|---|---|
| What is being transmitted | Message |
| The medium through which the message is being sent | Channel |
| The message is translated, and its meaning is generated | Decoding |
| The receiver responds to the message | Feedback |
| Anything which stops the message being transmitted as intended | Noise |

**133 A, B and C – Horizontal**

**D – Vertical**

Horizontal conflict occurs between groups or departments at the same level in the organisation while vertical conflict occurs at different levels of the organisation.

**134 A Reciprocity**

**B Liking**

**C Social proof**

Reciprocity means identifying what you want to achieve and what you need from the other person then considering what you may be able to offer them in return.

Liking means building relationships with those you want to influence so that they trust you.

Social proof means using the opinions of those already supporting you to influence others to join that support.

**135 C**

Non-verbal actions can vary between countries and cultures.

**136 The completed sentences are:**

**Tuckman** suggested that teams typically pass through several stages of development.

**Vaill** claimed that high-performance teams had several common characteristics.

**Belbin** suggested that a well-balanced group should contain nine identified character types.

**137 The correct matching is shown below:**

| | |
|---|---|
| Attendees talk too much | Chairperson should impose order |
| Objectives of the meeting are unclear | Agenda should be circulated before the meeting |
| Action points from previous meetings not carried out | Ensure action points agreed, and minutes of meeting are issued |
| Lack of enthusiasm at the meeting | Ensure the correct attendees are invited |

**138 C**

Persuasion is a stronger form of influence.

Persuasion is always direct.

Persuasion falls short of telling the other person what to do, the aim is to get their agreement.

**139 C**

S resigned because their employer's conduct was sufficient to be deemed to have terminated their employment contract. This is constructive dismissal.

**140 C**

Conflict reduction involves building on areas of agreement and on common objectives, and changing attitudes and perceptions of the parties involved. Techniques that can be used include compromises and concessions. These can be facilitated by independent third-party interventions, such as conciliation and arbitration.

## MANAGING PROJECTS

**141 D**

Time, cost and quality are primary project constraints. Other constraints include, for example, ethical, legal, environmental, and technological.

**142 The correct matching is shown below:**

| | |
|---|---|
| Work packages and Statements of work | To specify the work to be done for each activity and who will carry it out |
| Cost breakdown structure | To cost each element of the project |
| Work breakdown structure | To divide the work to be carried out into manageable pieces |
| Product breakdown structure | To identify the product purchases required for each activity |

**143 C**

Don't confuse 'configuration management' (tracking changes to project products, and hence product versions) and 'conformance management' (using inspection, quality control and quality assurance to ensure that the product/service meet the customer's specifications and requirements). While configuration management is also part of 'change management', this term implies a wider process of dealing with the need to amend projects in line with changes in user requirements, or difficulties of realising them in practice.

**144 A**

The first stage of the project life cycle (identification of a need) involves identifying a need, opportunity or problem. During this stage a feasibility study will be carried out. At the end of this phase the company will decide whether to proceed with the project, and if it does a PID (project initiation document) will be produced.

**145 A, C and E**

Development of a proposed solution is the project plan and performance enhancement will be the expected benefits of a project. Every project has constraints and although it is important to consider these, it is not possible to eliminate them.

**146 The correct matching is shown below:**

| | |
|---|---|
| Resource histogram | Helps with capacity planning |
| Critical path analysis | Identifies the activities that cannot overrun without delaying the overall project completion |
| PERT | Allows a calculation of contingency to be added to the project plan |
| Breakdown structures | Establishes the authority and responsibility for each part of the project |

**147 A, C and D**

Stakeholders, chain of command and scope would generally be sections in the project initiation document (PID).

**148 A, B and C**

Change control is used to identify, agree and communicate changes to the project. Risk management considers how risks associated with a project can be managed. Regular reporting helps monitor what has happened in the reporting period but will not eliminate deviations from the project plan.

**149 C**

In the PRINCE2 project organisational structure, the project assurance team fulfils this role. The project committee is also representative of user, executive and supplier interests, but its task is to provide senior input to project management. Project support is an optional set of administrative roles.

**150 The correct matching is shown below:**

1 Initiating

2 Planning

3 Controlling

4 Executing

5 Closing

**151 B**

The project steering committee is ultimately responsible for closing down a project. This may happen at the recommendation of the project manager.

**152 C**

The question defines a 'Work Breakdown Structure' (WBS). CBS is a Cost Breakdown Structure (a similar approach but applied to costs rather than tasks). CPA is Critical Path Analysis. PID is a project initiation document which is the output of the initiating phase of the project.

**153 C**

The project owner is the person for whom the project is being carried out. They are concerned with the scope and functionality of the project.

The project sponsor makes the yes/no decisions about the project, is responsible for approving the project plan and provides the funding for the project.

The project steering committee is ultimately responsible for closing down a project. This may happen at the recommendation of the project manager.

The project manager reports project progress to the project sponsor.

**154 D**

The scope of the project explains the boundaries of the project and exactly what is going to be delivered.

**155 C**

A project manager requires many skills, including negotiation, leadership, change management and problem solving amongst others but the project manager does not usually require specialist financial skills. Accountants involved in the project can provide these skills.

**156 D**

The team have been together for time and work successfully together. They respect C as the team leader. This suggests that the team are working at the performing stage of team development.

**The completed CPA for the project is:**

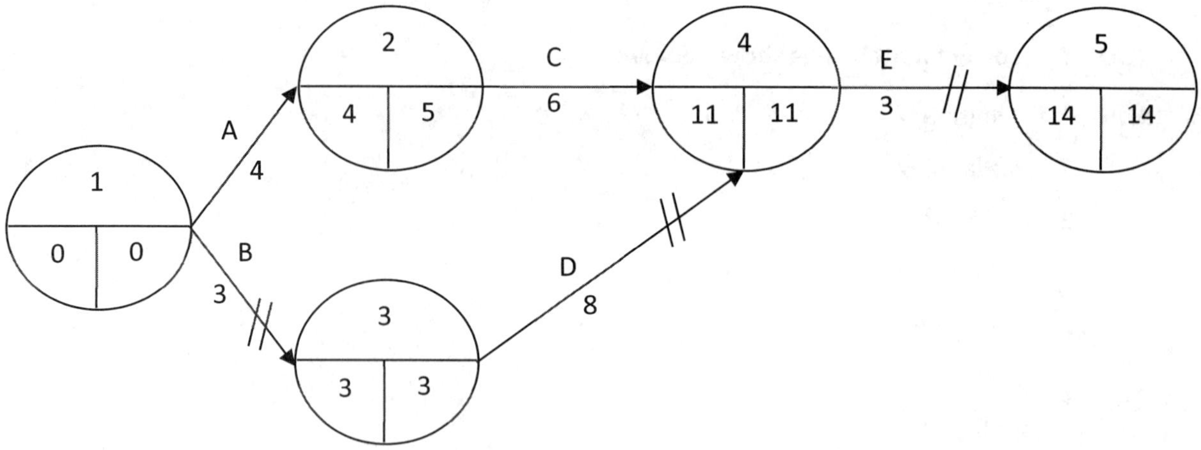


**157** The overall project duration is **14 months**

**158 B** – the critical activities are B, D and E

**159 A, B, D**

Specifying the work to be done for each package described is part of the work package (WP) whereas indicating who is responsible and when the work needs to be delivered is part of the statement of work (SOW). The product breakdown structure (PBS) is used to compare different suppliers.

**160 D**

The project sponsor makes the yes/no decisions about the project, is responsible for approving the project plan and provides the funding for the project. The project manager reports project progress to the project sponsor.

**161 C**

The initiation of the project need (identification of a need) will correspond with forming the project team.

**162 B**

A resource histogram is a component bar chart showing the number and mix of resources required each day (or other time unit) for the duration of a project.

A Gantt chart is a horizontal bar chart, where the length of the bar represents duration of an activity (whether planned or actual duration, or both, for comparison).

A network diagram is used to present the activities required for the project using arrows and nodes. It shows which activities must be done before others and highlights where activities can be delayed or done at the same time as other activities.

A work breakdown structure breaks down a project into manageable pieces and is an important starting point for planning a project.

**163 B**

A milestone is used to assess the status of the project. Milestones are key points in the project life cycle which give the project sponsor or steering committee an opportunity to review project progress.

A gate, which may also be a milestone, is a specific review point in the project which cannot be passed unless the performance of the project to that point has met predetermined performance standards.

A critical path is the chain of events that determines the overall duration of the project. Any delays to any activity on the critical path will delay the whole project.

PERT stands for project evaluation and review technique, and this is a technique used alongside critical path analysis to attempt to overcome uncertainties within the project time plan.

**164 D**

Technical feasibility investigates whether project requirements can be met using available material, technology and processes: i.e. is it possible? Economic feasibility investigates whether there will be a benefit that outweighs the cost: i.e. is it worthwhile? Social feasibility investigates whether the project fits with the culture and social organisation of the firm: i.e. **can** our people do this? Ecological feasibility investigates whether the project is environmentally sound and sustainable: i.e. **should** we do this?

**165 A, B and D**

The Project Management Body of Knowledge (PMBoK) describes nine key areas:

- Integration
- Scope
- Time
- Cost
- Quality
- Human Resources
- Communications
- Risk
- Procurement

**166 A**

Matrix structures have several advantages when used in companies which run a number of projects. It can improve lateral communication and cooperation between specialists as decision making needs to cut across divisional boundaries.

B is incorrect as matrix structures can make reporting to managers more difficult since employees can become confused by reporting to two mangers.

C is incorrect as matrix structures can lead to increased time spent in meetings as mangers need to discuss the prioritising of tasks.

D is incorrect as the matrix structure is most useful where a company runs a number of projects but where the projects have different start and end dates as the matrix structure can make it easier to reassign resources between projects.

**167 C**

There are 6 process areas in PRINCE2:

- Starting up a project
- Initiation
- Managing stage boundaries
- Controlling a stage
- Managing product delivery
- Project closure

**168 A**

A project sponsor usually makes key 'yes/no' decisions and provides the resources for a project.

The project manager is responsible for the successful delivery of the project objectives.

The project owner is the person for whom the project is being carried out.

The project customer (or user) is the person, or group of people, whose needs the project is attempting to satisfy.

**169** **A** **Senior user**

**B** **Project manager**

**C** **Stage team leader**

**D** **Project assurance team**

The completed diagram is shown below:

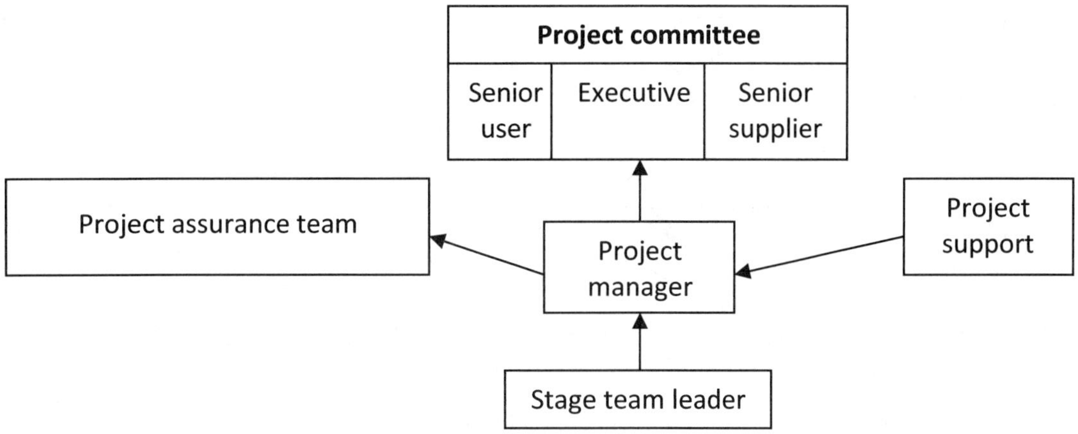


This is a useful diagram: note which way the reporting/authority arrows point. The project manager is the interface between the project committee (or board) and the stage team leaders. The project assurance team provides an independent 'lateral' view of how the project is progressing, reflecting the interests of the committee members. The project support roles provide administrative and communication activities.

**170** **C**

A, B and D would all normally be included in the final report. The extent to which the benefits defined in the original business case have been achieved (C) would not normally be included in the final report as this would not be able to be ascertained until a few months after the completion of the project.

**171** **C**

A, and D are benefits of resource histograms. B is a benefit of using project management software.

**172** **D**

Gantt charts will be of limited use when dealing with a relatively large project team. The more complex the team structure, the higher the likelihood of schedule delays. The other answer choices are advantages of Gantt charts.

**173** The float time on activity C is **8 days**

The completed CPA is shown below:

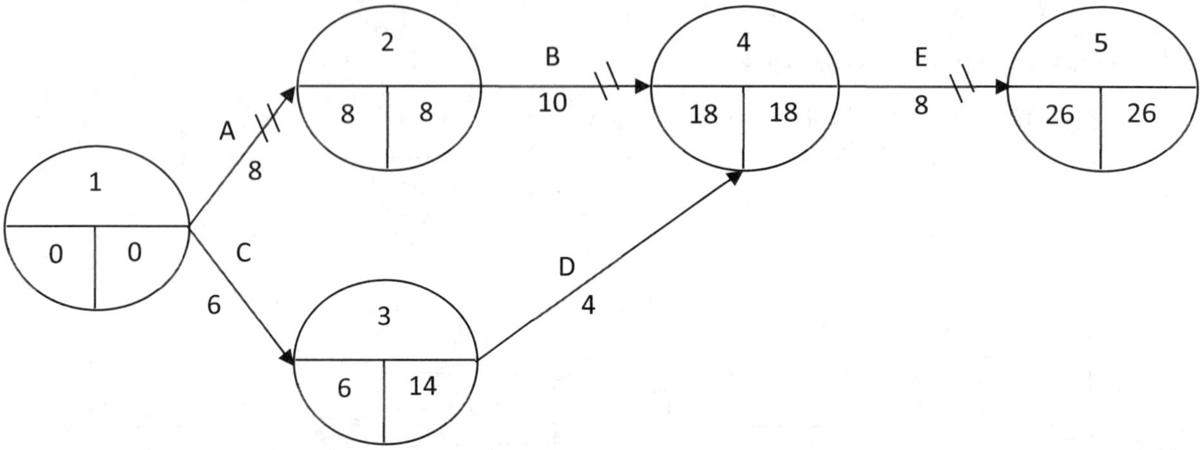


The float time is calculated as: Latest event time minus Earliest event time. For C this would be: 14 – 6 = 8 days

The critical path activities (A, B, E) have a zero float.

**174 B**

The scope of the project explains what should be included in the project deliverables. This must be agreed at the outset of the project before detailed planning takes place.

**175 A**

The correct order is identification of a need, development of a proposed solution, implementation, completion.

**176 A, C and E**

Option B is a key area of project management body of knowledge **(PMBOK)**.

Option D is a **key use** of project management software.

Option F is not an advantage. Project management software may have the ability to handle complexity but **does not reduce project complexity**.

**177 D**

Progress reporting is a control activity which should be carried out regularly by the project manager. The other items (A, B and C) would all specifically be included in configuration management.

**178 D**

Compromise is the most obvious approach to conflict management, but it does imply that both /all parties in the conflict must sacrifice something.

**179 C**

Team management is graded (9, 9). The other options are Country Club (1, 9), Task orientated (9, 1) and Impoverished (1, 1). Note that, in Blake and Mouton's model, concerns for task and people were not mutually exclusive: the 'best' style, according to them, is to have a high focus on both elements.

**180 The completed diagram is shown below:**

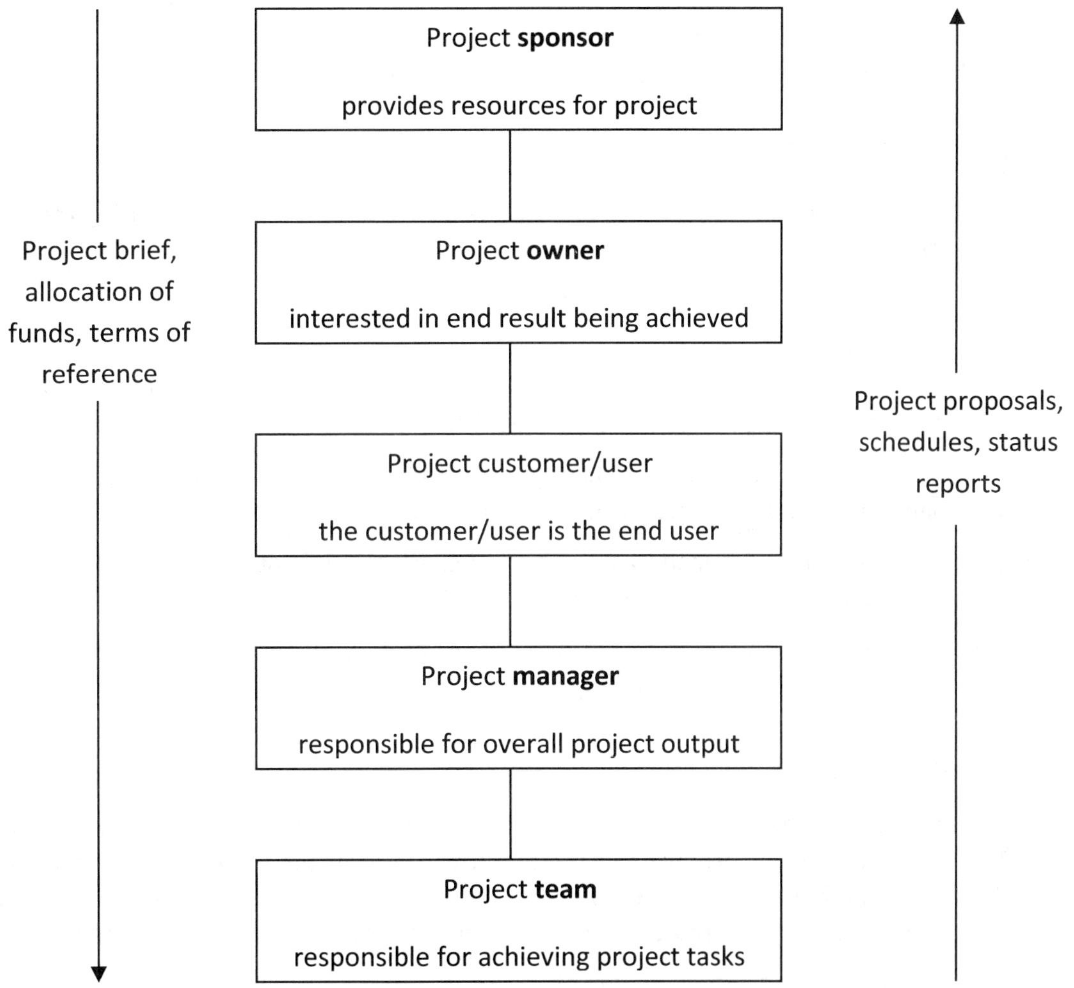


**181 D**

The carrying out of risk analysis is carried out as part of the initiating stage of the project lifecycle.

The other activities (A, B and C) would all be carried out during the executing stage.

**182 D**

A describes negotiation, B describes partnering and C describes compromise.

**183 C**

Tuckman suggested that all teams go through the following stages of development:

- Forming
- Storming
- Norming
- Performing
- Adjourning/Dorming

At the norming stage, standards of working are established, and ways of working are agreed.

**184 D**

A Gantt chart is a horizontal bar chart with the length of each bar representing the length of the activity.

**185 C**

Conformance management is concerned with compliance with technical specifications and would focus on items such as inspection, quality control and quality assurance.

Focus on items such as prioritising change requests, recording of changes and agreement of a change budget would suggest a change process.

Focus on items such as functional quality and client satisfaction measures would suggest a performance management system.

Focus on items such as access control over project records and version control for documentation would suggest configuration management.

**186 A, B and C**

The main control elements used within projects are project meetings and project reports. The feasibility study is produced at the initiation stage of the project to help management decide on whether the project is worth undertaking. Scenario planning and PERT are used at the planning stage of the project to consider the risk and uncertainty within the project.

**187 C**

The external review is an important review carried out at the end of the project. It is a review held with the customer to establish if the project had satisfied customer requirements.

Progress reports are an important technique used during the controlling of the project.

Gantt charts are used in planning the time requirements of the project during the planning stage.

PERT is used to take account of uncertainty and risk during the planning stage.

**188 B**

Progress review meetings should be regular, formal meetings involving the project manager, team members and the customer or steering committee. The purpose of these meetings is to provide an update on the project status and to identify any issues and action plans from that point.

Team meetings should also be held regularly between the project manager and the project team members. The object of these meetings is to keep all team members up to date with project progress.

Problem solving meetings are held on an ad hoc basis to deal with specific problems which have arisen in the project.

Business review meetings are held at the end of the project as part of the overall review of the project.

**189 D**

The Project Initiation Document (PID) will be produced during the 'identification of need' stage. Project scheduling is part of the planning phase, milestone reviews are part of implementation and control, and the completion report will be produced at the end of the lifecycle.

**190 C**

The critical path can be identified from the nodes. Where the earliest event time (EET) and the latest event time (LET) are the same, this indicates that there is no 'slack' in these activities and therefore the activities are on the critical path.

**191 B, C and E**

The slack on activities C and F is 13 weeks.

Activities A, B and C can start straight away and can be carried out at the same time. Activity D cannot start until after activity A is complete.

**192 C**

Risks with high likelihood and low impact are best managed by reduction. Reduction of risk can be achieved by implementing controls, or by taking alternative courses of action.

Risks with high likelihood and high impact should be avoided.

Risks with low likelihood and high impact should be transferred.

Risks with low likelihood and low impact should be accepted.

**193 B**

Buffering involves adding artificial slack into risky activities. It adds padding to the original estimates and allows for the fact that it is difficult to ensure that all stages and activities are carried out exactly as planned.

Scenario planning is another technique which can be used to take account of risk and uncertainty in projects. This involves the considering of one or more sets of circumstances that might occur within the project other than the most likely or expected set of circumstances.

Float refers to the extra time available for project activities which are not in the critical path.

PERT (project evaluation and review technique) uses a formula to calculate an expected time for each activity, considering a probable time, an optimistic time and a pessimistic time.

**194 D**

Contingency theory suggests that the effectiveness of various managerial practices, styles and techniques will vary according to the circumstances of the situation. The contingency theorists embrace all appropriate principles that enable managers to manage more effectively. Regardless of the organisational structure or the obstacles and opportunities they encounter, managers have some leeway in the choices they make and in the actions they initiate and they should be able to adapt their actions to suit the situation.

**195 A**

In the theory X model, people are seen as lazy and will work only if there is a direct link between efforts and rewards. A Theory Y manager would consider that all the other factors would motivate.

**196 B**

Project management software can help in managing the project's budget but cannot ensure that the project delivers within budget.

**197 A**

Most likely to be affected by change are the project budget and the project timescale.

**198 A, B and E**

C is incorrect. The matrix structure is commonly used in many industries, especially engineering, construction and consulting.

D is incorrect. The matrix structure is most useful where organisations regularly carry out multiple projects.

F is incorrect. A matrix structure is suitable for projects that are complex and expensive.

**199 A**

Risks with low likelihood and high impact should be transferred, for example by subcontracting the manufacture of key components to a specialist supplier.

Risks with low likelihood and low impact should be accepted. Risks with high likelihood and low impact are best managed by reduction. Risks with high likelihood and high impact should be avoided.

**200 B**

The project sponsor is responsible for the initiation of projects, approving project plans and making all major project decisions.